(co

the world.

We confess -
edged the com .ur
lives.

We acknowledge that God requires love. But we have not demonstrated the love of God to those suffering social abuses.

We acknowledge that God requires justice. But we have not proclaimed or demonstrated his justice to an unjust American society. Although the Lord calls us to defend the social and economic rights of the poor and the oppressed, we have mostly remained silent. We deplore the historic involvement of the church in America with racism and the conspicuous responsibility of the evangelical community for perpetuating the personal attitudes and institutional structures that have divided the body of Christ along color lines. Further, we have failed to condemn the exploitation of racism at home and abroad by our economic system.

We affirm that God abounds in mercy and that he forgives all who repent and turn from their sins. So we call our fellow evangelical Christians to demonstrate repentance in a Christian discipleship that confronts the social and political injustice of our nation.

We must attack the materialism of our culture and the maldistribution of the nation's wealth and services. We recognize that as a nation we play a crucial role in the im-

1

balance and injustice of international trade and development. Before God and a billion hungry neighbors, we must rethink our values regarding our present standard of living and promote more just acquisition and distribution of the world's resources.

We acknowledge our Christian responsibilities of citizenship. Therefore, we must challenge the misplaced trust of the nation in economic and military might—a proud trust that promotes a national pathology of war and violence which victimizes our neighbors at home and abroad. We must resist the temptation to make the nation and its institutions objects of near-religious loyalty.

We acknowledge that we have encouraged men to prideful domination and women to irresponsible passivity. So we call both men and women to mutual submission and active discipleship.

We proclaim no new gospel, but the gospel of our Lord Jesus Christ, who, through the power of the Holy Spirit, frees people from sin so that they might praise God through works of righteousness.

By this declaration, we endorse no political ideology or party, but call our nation's leaders and people to that righteousness which exalts a nation.

We make this declaration in the biblical hope that Christ is coming to consummate the Kingdom and we accept his claim on our total discipleship till he comes.

ORIGINAL SIGNERS

John F. Alexander
Joseph Bayly
Ruth L. Bentley
William Bentley
Dale Brown
James C. Cross
Donald Dayton
Roger Dewey
James Dunn
Daniel Ebersole
Samuel Escobar
Warren C. Falcon
Frank Gaebelein
Sharon Gallagher
Theodore E. Gannon
Art Gish
Vernon Grounds
Nancy Hardesty
Carl F. H. Henry
Paul Henry
Clarence Hilliard
Walden Howard
Rufus Jones
Robert Tad Lehe
William Leslie
C. T. McIntire

Wes Michaelson
David O. Moberg
Stephen Mott
Richard Mouw
David Nelson
F. Burton Nelson
William Pannell
John Perkins
William Petersen
Richard Pierard
Wyn Wright Potter
Ron Potter
Bernard Ramm
Paul Rees
Boyd Reese
Joe Roos
James Robert Ross
Eunice Schatz
Ronald J. Sider
Donna Simons
Lewis Smedes
Foy Valentine
Marlin Van Elderen
Jim Wallis
Robert Webber
Merold Westphal
John Howard Yoder

THE
CHICAGO
DECLARATION

Ronald J. Sider, Editor

Creation House

Carol Stream, Illinois

The essay "Prayer and Social Concern" by Paul Rees was
published in the Reformed Journal (January, 1974); the essay "Engagement—the Christian's Agenda" by Foy Valentine was published in the Reformed Journal (February
and March, 1974). Both essays copyright © 1974 by William B. Eerdmans Publishing Company. Reprinted by
permission.

Printed in the United States of America.

International Standard Book Number 0-88419-048-X
Library of Congress Catalog Card Number 74-82506

Contents

7

5 Reflections

Acknowledgements

The 1973 Thanksgiving Workshop on Evangelicals and Social Concern and the resulting Chicago Declaration flowed from the dreams, hard work, prayers, and courage of many people.

Four evangelical elder statesmen who had the courage and faith to risk working with young evangelical social activists deserve special recognition: Frank Gaebelein, Carl F. H. Henry, Rufus Jones, and Paul Rees. They contributed more than they realize to growing understanding, appreciation, and mutual trust between younger and older evangelicals concerned with social justice.

As coordinator, I want to express the strongest appreciation for the work of the other members of the planning committee. They all deserve to be listed as coeditors of this book: John Alexander (editor, *The Other Side*), Myron Augsburger (president, Eastern Mennonite College), Frank Gaebelein (headmaster emeritus, the Stony

Brook School and former coeditor, *Christianity Today*), Paul Henry (Calvin College), Rufus Jones (general director, Conservative Baptist Home Mission Society), David O. Moberg (chairman, department of sociology and anthropology, Marquette University), William Pannell (vice-president, Tom Skinner Associates), Richard Pierard (Indiana State University), Lewis Smedes (Fuller Theological Seminary), Jim Wallis (editor, *The Post-American*). In spite of very busy schedules, they invested many, many hours of time. They even paid their own travel expenses.

An expanded planning committee is busy developing additional activities. All profits from the sale of this book will be used to support these ongoing workshops and other programs designed to increase biblical social concern.

Introduction

An Historic Moment for Biblical Social Concern

Ronald J. Sider

"While the rest of American Protestantism was enjoying the annual festival of orgy and guilt, forty or so evangelical Christians were making their way to Chicago to take part in marathon discussions which could well change the face of both

Ronald J. Sider is the dean of Messiah College (Philadelphia Campus). He holds the B.A. from Waterloo Lutheran University and the M.A., B.D., and Ph.D. from Yale. He is a frequent contributor to religious journals and the author of Andreas Bodenstein von Karlstadt *(Brill, 1974). He coordinated the Thanksgiving Workshop on Evangelicals and Social Concern, and is chairman of an expanded committee, Evangelicals for Social Action, which is planning further workshops.*

religion and politics in America."[1] What prompts a secular newspaperwoman for the *Washington Post* to look to evangelical Christians with such expectancy?

An historic opportunity. I am convinced that at no time in the twentieth century have evangelicals confronted so momentous an opportunity and so weighty an obligation. This propitious moment results from a complex configuration of events both within and without evangelical Christianity. Internally, evangelicals are finally beginning to transcend the one-sidedness caused by the social gospel/fundamentalism controversy; they are learning (e.g., Key '73) to work cooperatively with biblical Christians in all the denominational traditions; and they are experiencing an intellectual renaissance, rapid growth, and new outbreaks of revival. Externally, liberal theology and its ecclesiastical bureaucracy are in serious trouble. In addition, the disruptive events of Vietnam and Watergate are freeing evangelicals from an automatic acceptance of traditional sociopolitical presuppositions.

How do each of these developments contribute to our present opportunity? We are all familiar

---

1. Marjorie Hyer, "Evangelicals: Tackling the Gut Issues," *Christian Century,* December 19, 1973, p. 1244. She also wrote two stories on the Thanksgiving Workshop for the *Washington Post* (Nov. 30, 1973, p. D17 and Dec. 28, 1973, p. C13).

with the way the liberalism/fundamentalism controversy in the early twentieth century resulted in the tragic loss of concern for social justice which had been so much a part of British and American evangelicalism in the eighteenth and nineteenth centuries.[2] What is exciting and important, however, is that evangelicals are beginning to transcend the unholy dichotomy of evangelism or social concern. The lonely pioneers such as Fred and John Alexander who began *The Other Side* (an evangelical social-action journal formerly called *Freedom Now*), Paul Rees, and David O. Moberg have been joined by others such as Tom Skinner and Leighton Ford. The forthright pleas for biblical social action at the Minneapolis Congress on Evangelism (1969) and Carl Henry's *Call For Evangelical Demonstration* (1971)[3] were signs that a new wind was blowing.

---

2. See David O. Moberg, *The Great Reversal: Evangelism Versus Social Concern* (Philadelphia: J.B. Lippincott, 1972), especially chap. 2. For previous centuries, see J. Wesley Brady, *England: Before and After Wesley* (London: Hodder and Stoughton, n.d.); Timothy L. Smith, *Revivalism and Social Reform* (New York: Harper Torchbooks, 1965); Gilbert H. Barnes, *The Anti-Slavery Impulse (1830-1844)* (New York: Harcourt, Brace and World, 1964); Earle E. Cairns, *Saints and Society* (Chicago: Moody, 1960).

3. Grand Rapids: Baker Book House. In a significant sense, Henry himself was one of the lonely pioneers, for his first book was a call for social concern: *The Uneasy Conscience of Modern Fundamentalism* (Grand Rapids: Eerdmans, 1947). Moberg, *The Great Reversal,* pp. 160 ff has a few pages on the emergence of recent social concern.

While a few journalists, evangelists, and scholars were laying the theoretical foundations, others were at work at the grass roots. There has been a flood of evangelical involvement in concrete social-action projects in the past decade. Black evangelical John Perkins defied organized bigotry and police brutality (he would have been lynched in 1971 if the FBI had not arrived at the last moment) to develop a vast program in education and health care in Mendenhall, Mississippi. Organized in 1969 by an interracial group of evangelicals, the Philadelphia Association of Christian Schools is providing quality education for a rapidly growing number of inner-city children. The Urban Life Center in Chicago, Westmont College's San Francisco program and Messiah College's inner-city campus in North Philadelphia reflect a growing emphasis on social concern in evangelical colleges.[4] One could mention similar evangelical activity in every part of the country.[5] The list of new concrete programs of social concern is long and growing. The point of course is not that evangelicals as a whole have already developed a balanced program directed to the needs of the whole man, but rather that they have made a significant beginning. A rapidly

---

4. For these programs, see Craig Ellison, ed., *The Urban Mission* (Grand Rapids: Eerdmans, 1974). See also my "Christian Cluster Colleges—Off to a Good Start," *Christianity Today,* May 24, 1974, pp. 12-16.

5. See for instance the March-April 1974 issue of *Inside* and Moberg, *The Great Reversal,* chap. 8.

growing movement of biblical social concern is emerging among evangelicals in the seventies. The moment when it reaches full flower may be at hand.

Not all was sweetness and light in the response to Key '73's ecumenical stance, for some conservative evangelicals refused to participate. But Key '73 did (in spite of less funding and consequently fewer projects than projected) broaden the contacts and spirit of cooperation between evangelical Christians in the mainline churches and those in the smaller denominations. In the original editorial in *Christianity Today* which finally resulted in Key '73, Carl F.H. Henry urged broad cooperation not just in evangelism, but also in other areas. Now that Key '73 has demonstrated the possibilities in one area, greater cooperative ventures in others including social action are more likely.

The signs of creative ferment and rapid growth among evangelicals are numerous. The continuing success of the Graham crusades, the Jesus Movement, and the more recent outbreaks of revival in many places all across the continent witness to the Spirit's continuing activity. In the last decade, while mainline seminaries were losing students, retrenching, and sometimes closing, evangelical seminaries such as Fuller, Trinity, Asbury, and Gordon-Conwell were experiencing phenomenal growth. Analogous developments occurred in Sunday school enrollments, church membership, religious publishing, and foreign missions.[6] As a result, it is increasingly recognized that evangelicals (perhaps numbering 40 million) are now in a majority in American Protestantism.[7] The potential influence for a more just society which these 40 million evangelicals could wield is massive.

In addition to these internal developments, the decline of theological liberalism and recent political developments also make the present moment particularly propitious for a new evangelicalism proclaiming and living the whole gospel for the whole man. Increasing criticism and decreasing giving and church attendance are causing painful retrenchment and deepening gloom in the more liberal denominations. Inadequate theology is certainly one factor in their decline. When liberalism neglected the fact that sin is deeper than social structures, that personal ethics are as important as social ethics, that societal improvements do not equal salvation, and that social restructuring will not usher in the Kingdom, it neglected fundamental biblical themes. The ever more rapid succession of new theologies—Bultmannianism, the "Death of God"

---

6. See for instance Donald G. Bloesch, *The Evangelical Renaissance* (Grand Rapids: Eerdmans, 1973), chap. 1.

7. One of the earlier secular magazines to note this was *Time* (Sept. 19, 1969, pp. 92,94). *Time* suggested 11.1 million Southern Baptists, 3.3 million other Baptists, 5.7 million Lutherans, 2.3 million in the Churches of Christ, 4.6 million Pentecostals, Wesleyans, and other small evangelical denominations, and 13 million in the mainline denominations.

theology, secular Christianity, the theology of hope, and the theology of liberation—has not provided a stable theological foundation. In short, liberal Christianity is in significant disarray.

Evangelical social activists, of course, dare not overlook the fact that prophetic social criticism by mainline churchmen has also contributed to the decline in their membership and revenues. As evangelicals speak out more and more against the structural injustice of American society, those whose economic self-interest is currently well served by the status quo will find other rationalizations for objecting. These defections, however, could be offset by the fact that there is a growing number of disenchanted liberal churchmen who are ready to search the Scriptures anew and listen attentively to evangelicals who demonstrate a balanced biblical concern for both social restructuring and individual conversion.

But, some observers of the current scene would interject, is not this flourishing evangelical majority a part of that conservative middle America which in recent years demanded, via the polling booth, a halt to further governmental activity designed to produce greater racial and economic equality? Are evangelicals not wedded to the status quo?[8] Perhaps not—at least not quite as

---

8. See, for instance, Robert G. Clouse, Robert D. Linder, and Richard P. Pierard, *The Cross and The Flag* (Carol Stream, Ill.: Creation House, 1972); and Richard V. Pierard. *The Unequal Yoke: Evangelical Christianity and Political Conservatism* (Philadelphia: J.B. Lippincott, 1970).

much since an obscure black security guard surprised the Watergate burglars. The Watergate scandal has provoked not just dismay but also deep reflection among many politically conservative evangelicals. As Harold O.J. Brown, associate editor of *Christianity Today,* and others indicate, some have concluded that evangelical Christians have been betrayed and exploited in recent years.[9] The extent of political corruption in high places horrifies and shocks many people who genuinely believed that justice, equality, and freedom were the goals, and honesty and due process the norms in Washington. But Watergate is forcing evangelicals to reexamine many fundamental assumptions about the supposed justice of governmental policy and practice both at home and abroad.

The result, of course, may be shocked withdrawal into the pygmy world of personal piety. Conservative Christians may conclude that since even "law and order" administrations are astonishingly corrupt, politics is too dirty for devout believers. They may forsake the political arena in droves.

---

9. See, for instance, Harold O.J. Brown, "Restive Evangelicals," *National Review,* XXVI (1974), 193: "A number of evangelical spokesmen privately indicate that they feel themselves betrayed by Nixon, whom they had accepted, if not as an evangelical, at least as a God-fearing and essentially honest man." See also (Republican) Paul Henry's comment apropos Nixon and Watergate: "The evangelical community has been exploited terribly." *Christian Century,* Dec. 19, 1973, p. 1245.

But another reaction is also possible. Precisely because the Watergate revelations have hopelessly tarnished the image of trusted political heroes and their political slogans, Watergate may free the evangelical community (which, by and large, has been a part of middle America) to take a new, far more critical look at all aspects of American society. The shock waves from Watergate may do what volumes of radical social criticism failed to do: raise fundamental questions about the justice of the socioeconomic status quo. If at this historic moment of socio-political uncertainty, questioning and flux, evangelicals can turn and hear with a new freshness and fewer preconceptions the explosive prophetic call for social justice contained in that Bible which they genuinely accept as God's authoritative revelation, then indeed they may change the face of politics in America.

Our concern, of course, must not be power but rather faithfulness to God's word. If our aim is to seize for the new evangelical majority the power, prestige and political influence formerly enjoyed by liberal churchmen in previous decades, then we deserve ignominious failure. What matters is faithfulness to the biblical word we cherish and to the risen Lord we worship as true God and follow as perfect Example. Since he called us (Matthew 25) to minister to himself by identifying with the poor and changing oppressive social structures, we can do no other and remain faithful disciples.

Evangelicals today face an historic opportunity. Their internal growth and developing cooperation with biblical Christians in all denominations at a time when liberal theology is in eclipse makes them a powerful new majority in American Protestantism. And the resurgence of biblical social concern within evangelical ranks plus the fundamental rethinking prompted by recent political developments raises the genuine possibility that their message to the world will be a biblical message of concern for the needs of the whole man.

Such a hope, however, may be at best optimistic and at worst incredibly naive. Certainly a dispassionate sociological analysis would indicate that middle-class evangelicals are unlikely to transcend their comfortable existence as part of the socioeconomic status quo in the richest nation on earth. But surely it is not too much to hope that precisely those Christians who abhor Marxist economic determinism and believe that the supernatural power of the risen Lord Jesus is now at work in regeneration and sanctification will be able, at least to some significant extent, to defy society's call for conformity and follow the biblical call for identification with the poor and oppressed. I agree with Carl Henry's stubborn optimism in his *Call for Evangelical Demonstration:* "If Bible-believing Christians can wade against the secular stream by mass evangelistic crusades aimed to rescue otherwise doomed sinners, they can summon enough courage and concern in public—at least I am convinced they can, and will, if fully aroused to the urgency of these times—to stand against the culture in majestic witness to the holy commandments of God."[10] By God's grace it is possible for evangelicals to respond faithfully to the historic opportunity of the present hour.

The obligation, of course, is as awesome as the challenge. For better or worse, evangelicals will exercise the dominant Protestant influence in the next decade. If at this moment of unparalleled influence they proclaim a truncated message focused only on personal salvation, then there will be an inevitable resurgence of liberal theology preoccupied with an equally one-sided concern for changing social structures. And evangelicals will have themselves to blame for failing to declare the full counsel of God to the whole man.

It was with deep awareness of the extent both of the opportunity and the obligation presented by this convergence of events that a group of evangelicals began to ponder the possibility of assembling a number of evangelical leaders to consult together and to seek the Lord for guidance. The Chicago Declaration was the result.

The Thanksgiving Workshop. Who should be invited? The planning committee[11] decided to

---

10. Preface, p. 7.

11. **John Alexander,** editor, *The Other Side;* **Myron Augsburger,** president, Eastern Mennonite College; **Frank Gaebelein,** headmaster emeritus, The Stony Brook School,

limit participants to those who were "evangelical." (Definitions are always slippery, but Harold Ockenga's definition in *Christianity Today* is useful: An evangelical is one who believes, on the basis of the Bible, which is the inspired, authoritative Word of God and hence the norm for faith and practice, the basic doctrines of historic Christianity—the deity of Christ, the sinfulness of man, justification by faith alone through Christ's death on the Cross, and regeneration.)[12] It hoped to avoid just a token representation of evangelical blacks and women. It wanted to include both Northerners and Southerners, both evangelical elder statesmen and younger, more "radical" evangelical voices. Since a majority of the 40 million evangelicals are in groups not associated with the National Association of Evangelicals, it was crucial to include evangelicals both from mainline denominations such as the Episcopal church and also from the

---

and former coeditor, *Christianity Today;* **Paul Henry,** department of political science, Calvin College; **Rufus Jones,** general director, Conservative Baptist Home Mission Society; **David O. Moberg,** chairman, department of sociology and anthropology, Marquette University; **William Pannell,** vice-president, Tom Skinner Associates; **Richard Pierard,** professor of history, Indiana State University; **Ronald J. Sider,** acting director, Messiah College (Philadelphia Campus), coordinator, Thanksgiving Workshop; **Lewis Smedes,** professor, Fuller Theological Seminary; **Jim Wallis,** editor, *The Post-American.*

12. Harold J. Ockenga, "Resurgent Evangelical Leadership," *Christianity Today,* Oct. 10, 1960, pp. 11-14.

more than 11 million Southern Baptists, the several million Missouri Synod Lutherans, and the more than 2 million persons in the Churches of Christ.

The planning committee invited persons from all these groups: evangelical elder statesmen such as Carl F.H. Henry, editor for many years of *Christianity Today,* and Paul Rees, vice-president-at-large of World Vision; younger voices such as Sharon Gallagher, editor of the Jesus Movement paper *Right On,* and C.T. McIntire, son of the famous fundamentalist preacher; black evangelicals such as William Bentley, president of the National Black Evangelical Association, and John Perkins, director of a highly successful evangelistic-social action program in Mississippi; leading voices for evangelical women such as Nancy Hardesty, formerly an assistant editor at *Eternity;* persons from the historic peace churches, such as John Howard Yoder, until recently president of Mennonite Biblical Seminary; Southern Baptists such as Foy Valentine, executive secretary of the Christian Life Commission of the Southern Baptist Convention; and Missouri Synod Lutheran James C. Cross.

In recent decades, evangelical leaders have not come together very often, if at all, to devote three full days exclusively to the discussion of biblical social concern. Would these busy persons, the planning committee wondered, have the time and interest to come? Would they sacrifice their

Thanksgiving vacation? The enthusiastic response to the letters of invitation quickly dispelled that doubt.

But could such a diverse group of persons, who certainly represented a wide range of sociopolitical viewpoints despite their common evangelical commitment, agree on anything significant apropos biblical social concern? Was it naive to suppose that a new consensus on the need for far more extensive identification with the poor and oppressed was emerging among evangelicals? No one could answer this question with certainty. The planning committee could only hope and pray and wait for the Thanksgiving weekend.

On Friday, November 23, 1973, about fifty persons assembled in the dingy surroundings of the YMCA Hotel on Chicago's South Wabash Street.[13] The life and sounds of the inner city

---

13. In addition to those just mentioned in the text and those on the planning committee (see note 11), the following participants were present: Joseph Bayly, vice-president, David C. Cook Publishing Co.; Ruth Bentley, University of Illinois Medical Center and Trinity College; Dale Brown, former moderator, Church of the Brethren; Betty Danielson, social worker, Minneapolis; Donald Dayton, vice-chairman, Commission on Social Concerns, Christian Holiness Assn.; Roger Dewey, editor, *Inside;* James M. Dunn, executive secretary, Texas Baptist Christian Life Commission; Samuel Escobar, general director, Inter-Varsity Christian Fellowship—Canada; Theodore E. Gannon, chairman, Social Concern Commission, National Association of Evangelicals; Vernon Grounds, president, Conservative Baptist Seminary; Clarence Hilliard, pastor, Circle Church, Chicago; Walden Howard, editor, *Faith at Work;* William Leslie, pastor, LaSalle Street Church, Chicago; Wes Michaelson, executive assistant to Senator Hatfield;

punctuated lofty theorizing with sharp reminders of the harsh reality of racism and economic injustice. (Just as Paul Henry solemnly declared that evangelicals dare no longer remain silent in the face of glaring social evil, a gunshot rang through the hall!) The medium, the planning committee hoped, would help convey the message. If evangelicals seriously intend to acknowledge the existence of a billion hungry neighbors, then that concern will shape their entire lifestyle, including the settings in which they hold their conferences.

The workshop began with three major presentations. Noted black evangelist and lecturer William Pannell focused the problem and posed the challenge in a hard-hitting talk (a choice sentence of which made *CBS Evening News*) on "Evangelicals and Social Concern: The Present

---

Stephen Mott, professor, Gordon-Conwell Divinity School; Richard Mouw, department of philosophy, Calvin College; F. Burton Nelson, professor, North Park Theological Seminary; William J. Petersen, executive editor, *Eternity;* Clark Pinnock, professor, Trinity Evangelical Divinity School; Wes Pippert, United Press International, Washington office; Wyn Potter; Bernard Ramm, professor, American Baptist Seminary of the West; James Robert Ross, professor, Lincoln Christian Seminary; Eunice Schatz, director, Urban Life Center, Chicago; Marlin Van Elderen, editor-in-chief, Eerdmans Publishing Co.; Robert Webber, editor-in-chief, Creation House; Merold Westphal, department of philosophy, Yale University. Also at the conference were several others who played important roles: Dan Ebersole, my energetic assistant; Marcia and Tad Lehe from Wheaton, who did the clerical work; and Boyd Reese and Joe Roos of the *Post-American,* who were in charge of transportation.

and the Future" (see chapter one). John Howard Yoder urged the participants to transcend their several hermeneutical traditions in order to hear afresh "The Biblical Mandate" (see chapter four). In a moving meditation on "Prayer and Social Concern" (see chapter three), Paul Rees challenged the assembled participants to immerse their social concern in prayer.

Lucid analysis and a call for prayer, however, do not necessarily produce immediate consensus and tranquil dialogue. When we gathered to evaluate the carefully prepared first draft of the declaration, the lid blew off. The black participants sharply attacked the planning committee for including only one black in the decision-making process. Rejecting the proposed statement on racism, they offered an alternative drawn up "over turnip greens and ham hocks for atmosphere."

With this issue far from settled, a second voice of protest immediately appeared. Pleading for "the other half" of the evangelical church, Nancy Hardesty urged the largely male gathering to take the issue of women's rights seriously and include more than the one word on sexism in the proposed draft. Evangelicals, she suggested, are at about the same place on the role of women as white Christians were vis-a-vis blacks when they perceived the decisive word on black/white relations in the alleged curse of Ham.

As if all this were not enough, John Howard Yoder rose to plead the cause of a third oppressed group in evangelical circles—the historic peace churches—and protest the absence of any statement on war. "Blacks have a paragraph they can redo; women have a word they can redo; but there is nothing at all about war. It contains something about the military-industrial complex being bad for the budget, but nothing about it being bad for the Vietnamese."

After these and other lengthy objections to the style and content, we finally concluded the day exhausted. Even the more optimistic now questioned the probability of any final consensus. Many eagerly sought out their small rooms in the Y for prayer and badly needed rest. It was symbolic of the prevailing mood that those who felt the need for a late snack traveled the dark streets in two separate groups. One was all white, the other all black, and they vented their frustration in angry separation.

Next morning a new drafting committee set to work to prepare a second draft of the declaration.[14] When it was ready, the participants met in plenary session for most of Saturday afternoon and evening to evaluate the new statement. The debate was vigorous and lively. Sometimes it was also humorous. When an older evangelical pronounced the idea of mutual sub-

---

14. The drafting committee was composed of John Alexander, William Bentley, Frank Gaebelein, Paul Henry, Stephen Mott, William Pannell, Bernard Ramm, Lewis Smedes, and Jim Wallis. Whatever literary polish the declaration has is due in large part to Frank Gaebelein.

mission by men and women "innocuous," a young evangelical (male) retorted, with a mixture of banter and impertinence, "Perhaps you have never tried it!" As blacks and whites, men and women, younger evangelicals and older evangelicals debated with and listened to each other throughout the afternoon, they discovered—somewhat to everyone's surprise—that there was a solid foundation of agreement. In spite of continuing substantial differences on, say, the ideal economic system, all agreed that present economic structures both here and abroad are racist and unjust.

It was with a growing sense of excitement and unity that we approved one section after another. By the end of the evening, we were together on almost all points of the final document. And when it was again time for a late evening snack, one group of black and white brothers and sisters went out to enjoy soul food together.

On Sunday morning, after some additional debate on a few remaining items, the Chicago Declaration of Evangelical Social Concern was approved unanimously. A deep sense of the presence and guidance of the risen Lord pervaded the room. "The Doxology" seemed the only fitting response. As we stood and sang together, we expressed both a prayer of profound thanks for the agreement He had created and a passionate prayer that the Chicago Declaration might in some small way be an instrument to assist "all creatures here below" to praise Father, Son and Holy Ghost.

To sign the Chicago Declaration required considerable courage for some. One older evangelical leader, who had experienced increasing alienation and isolation in recent years because of his forthright demand for more social concern among evangelicals, felt uncertain.[15] He first affixed and then removed his signature. But after a few minutes of inner anguish, he concluded that he must support the call for greater evangelical social concern, whatever the cost. After making his painful decision, he and one of the youngest men present expressed their common faith and concern with a warm embrace.

That embrace symbolized what had happened. Younger evangelicals, whose increasing dismay at the lack of evangelical social concern had been approaching despair, discovered a surprising degree of agreement (despite many differences on specific issues) on the part of elder evangelical statesmen. And those who were younger proved ready to listen to those with more years of experience. Just as significant as this bridging of the generation gap was the bridging of racial, sexual, and denominational gaps as well. Because of a common commitment to the lordship of Jesus Christ and the authority of Scripture, an extremely diverse group of evangelical leaders

---

15. Paul Henry, who chaired the sessions on the declaration, had made it very clear at the beginning that those who at the end might feel it advisable not to sign should not feel under pressure to do so.

had produced an historic statement on evangelical social concern.

That evangelism and social concern are inseparable and that individual and structural sin are equally abhorrent to Jahweh are among the more important theological affirmations of the Chicago Declaration. Conservative Christians have always condemned pot, pubs, and pornography, but they have expressed less holy horror in the face of institutional racism and oppressive economic systems. The Chicago Declaration, however, indicates that biblical repentance and conversion will entail confession of and turning away from all types of sin, and faithful discipleship will involve confronting social and economic injustice just as much as, say, individual acts of adultery or theft. Consequently it is not just that evangelism and social concern are both important, but rather that they are inseparable. Evangelistic proclamation is fully biblical only when it calls for repentance from all types of sins and urges a biblical discipleship in which all relationships, both personal and societal, are transformed. And prophetic social criticism is fully biblical only when it announces both that participation in structural evil is a damnable sin against God Almighty and also that divine forgiveness is bestowed on those who repent and turn from all their sins.

The workship had not achieved all the original goals. Because of the time required for discussion and approval of the declaration, there was less time for evaluation of concrete action proposals than originally intended.[16] But a theoretical foundation grounded in biblical faith had been laid, and an expanded planning committee was assigned the task of calling a second meeting to be devoted to specific action proposals. After Foy Valentine led in the closing worship service (see chapter two for his sermon), we parted with the conviction that the Chicago Declaration would provide a new emphasis on and visibility for evangelical social concern.

Reaction to the Chicago Declaration. Reaction in the secular press was prompt. *Chicago Sun-Times* writer Roy Larson declared: "Some day American church historians may write that the most significant church-related event of 1973 took place last week at the YMCA Hotel on S. Wabash."[17] There also were stories in the *Washington Post*, Cleveland's *Plain Dealer,* and the scores of dailies that carry Associated Press columnist George Cornell. The secular press was struck by the fact that evangelical Christians were stressing the importance of social concern just when liberal Christianity was easing up on social

---

16. The small amount of available time permitted only brief consideration of the few that were approved and precluded any consideration in plenary session of most of the action proposals presented. The 1974 workshop will focus on concrete proposals.

17. "Historic Workshop: Evangelicals Do U-turn, Take on Social Problems," *Chicago Sun-Times,* December 1, 1973.

action.[18] They also noted that "this new concern is more enduring than that of the liberals because it is more strongly grounded on biblical imperatives."[19]

In the religious press, of course, there has been a host of news stories, editorials and reprints of the Chicago Declaration. In spite of minor objections, a *Christianity Today* editorial pronounced the Chicago Declaration "admirably forthright and timely." "The basic thrust is absolutely biblical." The editorial added that "these issues have been addressed innumerable times, but perhaps never before in such clear and concise terms by so representative an assembly of American evangelicals."[20] In a ringing guest editorial in *Eternity* ("Evangelicals of America, Arise!"), Paul Henry called on evangelicals to implement the Chicago Declaration by producing contemporary counterparts to Wilberforce and Shaftesbury.[21] Positive evaluations appeared in *Christian Century, Christianity and Crisis,* and

---

18. See Alma Kaufman, "Evangelicals Get Cue on Social Concerns," *The Plain Dealer,* December 1, 1973, C2, and the places mentioned in note 19.

19. From George Cornell's syndicated column which appeared in scores of papers. See, for instance, *The Morning Call,* Allentown, Pa., December 1, 1973 or the *Tulsa Daily World,* Nov. 30, 1973.

20. *Christianity Today,* December 21, 1973, p. 24.

21. *Eternity,* February, 1974, pp. 12, 71, 72.

numerous denominational magazines.[22]

Congregations, denominational commissions, and interdenominational evangelical associations are discussing the Chicago Declaration. The Board of Bishops of the Free Methodist Church discussed the declaration, and several bishops wrote and asked to be identified with it.[23] The Christian Life Commission of the Baptist General Convention of Texas, the social-action agency for the 1.9 million Texas Southern Baptists, officially endorsed the declaration.

Aware that there were thousands of persons in the swelling movement of biblical social concern all around the country who would like to identify with the Chicago Declaration, it was decided to invite Christians who genuinely agreed with the declaration to become cosigners. Again the response has been enthusiastic. Cosigners include Leighton Ford, vice-president of the Billy Graham Association; black evangelist Tom Skinner; Oregon Senator Mark Hatfield; author

---

22. For the *Christian Century*, see note 1. John H. Yoder published an evaluative article, "The Spirit in the Windy City" in *Christianity and Crisis*, XXXIV (1974), 23-25. See also the January-February issue of *Inside*, the April issue of *Faith at Work*, and the February issue of *Reformed Journal*. Also James Robert Ross, "Evangelicals and Social Concern" in *Christian Standard*, February 3, 1974, pp. 9,10. Not everyone, of course, was pleased. See, for instance, the editorial in *The Banner*, Jan. 11, 1974, p. 4.

23. Bishops Myron F. Boyd, Paul N. Ellis, and W. Dale Cryderman.

Elton Trueblood; renowned Church of the Nazarene historian Timothy Smith; Christian Holiness Association President Henry Ginder; National Association of Evangelicals President Myron F. Boyd; and Young Life President William Starr.[24] Letters from persons eager to identify with the Chicago Declaration as cosigners arrive every day. They come from pastors from Georgia to Massachusetts; from young evangelicals who shout "Praise God for your action!" and tell of the way the declaration has encouraged them; from older evangelical statesmen like Latin American Mission's general director, Horace Fenton, Jr., who recalls "the time, not too many years ago, when an evangelical who said these things would have felt like a lone voice crying in the wilderness."[25] (Individuals, congregations, and other church bodies are still welcome to record their endorsement.)[26] The re-

---

24. A few additional cosigners are: Episcopalian Peter C. Moore, executive director, FOCUS; Robert J. Eells, executive secretary of the Christian Government Movement; Richard H. Bube, editor of *The Journal of the American Scientific Affiliation;* James W. Sire, editor, Inter-Varsity Press; Donn M. Gaebelein, headmaster, The Stony Brook School; Irwin Reist, chairman of the division of philosophy and religion, Houghton College; Arthur Holmes, chairman of the philosophy department, Wheaton College; Robert B. Munger, professor of evangelism, Fuller Theological Seminary; Ronald Enroth, chairman of the sociology department, Westmont College.

25. Horace L. Fenton Jr. to R.J. Sider, Dec. 8, 1973.

26. Write to Ronald J. Sider, coordinator, Thanksgiving

sponse to the Chicago Declaration signifies a change of historic magnitude in the evangelical community.

A few suggestions for the future. What is needed to keep this rapidly growing movement thoroughly biblical? In our theology, our rhetoric, and especially in the new structures which must of necessity emerge to give expression to the growing movement of biblical social concern, we must avoid a new cleavage between "evangelists" and "social prophets." Evangelicals who have been most involved with evangelism and evangelicals who have come to emphasize social concern very strongly must discover new ways to listen and learn together. We simply cannot afford the carnal luxury of shouting stereotyped caricatures of each other across the airwaves and printed page. On the other hand, honest brotherly criticism must continue. Somehow we must talk, pray, debate, and read the Word together until biblical social concern is an integral part of our evangelism and the proclamation of forgiveness through the Cross is integral to our prophetic social criticism. Only then can we faithfully proclaim the whole gospel for the whole man.

Workshop, Messiah College, 2026 North Broad St., Philadelphia, Pa. 19121. Free copies of the Chicago Declaration are available.

That many other things are needed is obvious—thousands of new local social-action projects developed by evangelicals, further theological discussion of the relationship between Christ and culture, more mechanisms for cooperative efforts in biblical social concern, more national and regional conferences and workshops on biblical social concern, more thoroughly competent analyses by Christian economists and political scientists of the character and extent of structural, institutionalized evil and possible political remedies.

The one thing needful, however, at this moment in time may very well be something which should have been—but seems not to be—obvious from our pietist heritage.[27] The most pressing agenda item for evangelical social activists in the seventies may very well be a renewed emphasis on prayer.

Such a suggestion may seem strange. Secular theologians may be heretical at this point, but of course we evangelicals certainly know that prayer is important! But do not our actions—especially in the case of evangelical social activists—rather often belie our words?

An increasing number of evangelicals understand clearly that biblical spirituality necessarily includes a profound sensitivity to social as well as personal evil and a passionate commitment to social justice. But have we done an

---

27. For a good discussion of evangelicalism's pietist heritage, see Bloesch, *The Evangelical Renaissance,* chap. 5.

equally adequate job of appropriating the central and profound role of prayer?

I have talked recently with many younger evangelical activists who, although their theology, work, and leadership are outstanding, nevertheless confess a deep deficiency in their understanding and practice of prayer. There is a genuine problem here that must be faced. When we see a situation that requires action, we find it far more natural to call together a committee and begin mapping out a strategy for action than to anguish before the Lord in extended prayer. (And extended prayer involves more than a perfunctory, introductory thirty-second invocation while the last persons straggle into the meeting.) How many of us find it easier to keep up with current politics each day than to spend equal time talking to the King? And when we do force ourselves to our knees, the result is too often empty words that "never to heaven go."

Why? Perhaps modern secularism has crept into our thinking more than we suspect. We certainly oppose the philosophical naturalist who rejects belief in the miraculous; we self-consciously affirm a supernatural world-view.[28] But has the secular rejection of miracles so affected us that extended prayer for divine guidance and intervention is no longer our daily

---

28. For one aspect of this issue which relates to historical methodology, see my "The Historian, The Miraculous, and Post-Newtonian Man," *Scottish Journal of Theology,* XXV (1972), 309-19.

practice and automatic response to new situations and needs?

The teaching and example of our Lord and the whole history of the Church challenge our secular instincts at this point. The Gospels repeatedly depict Jesus in prayer. He anguished at great length before the Father before his final confrontation with the religious and political establishment of his day.

Thielicke has said of Martin Luther that he prayed four hours each day "not despite his busy life, but because only so could he accomplish his gigantic labors."[29] Charles Finney, who combined extensive anti-slavery crusading with his role as one of the most prominent preachers in nineteenth-century revivalism, insisted that long intercessory prayer was always a part of revival: "Go and inquire among the obscure members of the church, and you will always find that someone had been praying for a revival and was expecting it—some man or woman had been agonizing in prayer."[30] In our own day, the Billy Graham organization has immersed its crusade preparations and activities in prayer. One suspects, in fact, that we evangelical social activists may have a lot more to learn from Graham

---

29. Quoted in Elton Trueblood, *The New Man for Our Time* (New York: Harper, 1970), pp. 66,67.

30. Charles G. Finney, *Lectures on Revivals of Religion* (New York: Revell, 1868), p. 30.

about prayer, among other things, than we are willing to admit.

Certainly the terrible social evils in our world cry out for action now. We dare not delay. Biblical Christians will challenge and oppose the rampant racism, economic exploitation, and militarism of America and the world. But are we not unbiblical if the first and constant component of our social action is not passionate, intercessory prayer that the Lord of the universe will use our efforts as he wills for the sake of justice? Are we not naive if we suppose that evangelical social activists will be any more effective than were liberals unless we totally immerse our concern and activity in prayer to the Father?

In short, the first agenda item for evangelical social activists in the seventies is prayer. We need to ask our Lord (and perhaps our less activist brothers?) to teach us how to pray for hours the way Jesus, Luther, and Wesley did. We need to beg the Lord to send us the spirit and practice of prayer that accompanied the great revivals which swept across the country in previous times. The numerous small prayer cells of the great revivals could also become a regular component—indeed, they could become the trademark—of evangelical social action in the seventies.

Should we spend at least as much time in prayer each day as we do keeping up with current events? Are we too sophisticated (and unspiritual?) to make our conferences and workshops on social ethics a little more like the old camp meetings where Christians interceded all night (like Jesus) for the radicalizing, revolutionary presence of the Spirit? In our committee meetings devoted to mapping out strategy for action, should we as a rule of thumb devote at least half as much time to seeking guidance from the King in prayer as we do in asking for insight from committee members?

Is it too much to hope that prayer might become the trademark of biblical social action in the seventies? Could we become known as the people who not only do the necessary research but also pray together for hours before we confront the city's zoning board with its racist policies? Could we become known as the people who pray all night before urging our denominational mission boards to invest large sums of money and personnel in inner-city programs run by black evangelicals? Could there be tens of thousands of local evangelical groups all across the country which would combine the most sophisticated socioeconomic analyses of institutionalized evil in existing societal structures with constant, intercessory prayer? Can we totally immerse our social action in prayer?

I believe that can happen. If it does, then there is every reason to expect that the Lord of history may repeat in our day what he accomplished through British and American evangelicals in the eighteenth and nineteenth centuries. Wilberforce and his fellow evangelicals ended the slave trade and then slavery throughout the British Empire. By obtaining important new social legislation apropos slavery, child labor, prison reform, etc., they significantly reshaped British society. In the United States, evangelicals such as Finney and Theodore Weld played a crucial role in the development of the abolitionist movement.[31] We should proceed with the joyous expectation that evangelicals will transcend their one-sidedness of recent decades and use their present power to demand greater justice for the poor and oppressed.

At the end of her analysis of the Chicago Declaration in the *Christian Century,* Marjorie Hyer observed:

> There are some reasons to believe that the course of history in recent years may have prepared a fertile seedbed among this country's evangelicals for the kind of ideas and concerns raised in the declaration .... If 40 million evangelicals in this country should start taking seriously all those problems that every religious convention resolutionizes about—well, it boggles the mind to think what could happen.[32]

Well-known church historian Martin E. Marty of the University of Chicago has expressed equal enthusiasm. He began a lengthy analysis of the Chicago Declaration with the assertion that the "formula for the most durable combination in modern Christian social ethics [is] biblical or doc-

---

31. See note 2 above.

32. *Christian Century,* Dec. 19, 1973, p. 1245.

trinal conservatism plus social vision and passion." He concluded his discussion with words of high expectation tinged with lingering doubt:

> If the movement sustains itself long enough to have engagements with the churches that produced its leaders, we may see something more significant than the now-passing "Jesus Freakism" or the ongoing pentecostal-charismatic movements. Out of this, people might be fed, the law might be rendered justly, and America might relocate itself in the world. One can dream.[33]

Is that too optimistic a dream?

I believe that evangelicals can indeed rise to the challenge of the present hour and proclaim and live the whole word of God for the whole man. But that will not happen merely through learned seminars and important declarations, no matter how sophisticated the analysis and how distinguished the participants. That will only happen through much prayer.

---

33. Martin E. Marty, *Context: A Commentary on the Interaction of Religion and Culture,* March 15, 1974, pp. 1,6.

Evangelicals and Social Concern: The Present and the Future

William Pannell

It is of interest to me that we are holding this conference in Illinois, for as you know, the center of population of the United States, according to the last decennial census, is downstate in a soybean field 5.3 miles east-southeast of Mascoutah, not far from Saint Louis.

And if the population center is in Illinois, so also is much of the tradition and institutional life of evangelicalism. Most of us have made some pilgrimage to these shrines for Bible conferences or the pursuit of Christian education. And not far from this hotel is the most successful evangelical

William Pannell, vice-president of Tom Skinner Associates, is an evangelist and campus lecturer. One of the first black graduates of Fort Wayne Bible College, he is the author of My Friend the Enemy *(Word, 1967), a regular columnist for* The Other Side, *and the author of numerous magazine articles.*

social-welfare program in America—the Pacific Garden Mission.

The issue joined. We have chosen to speak about the present and the future of evangelical social concern. I do not find this an easy task. In the first place, what is an evangelical? I was tempted to define that word, but thought better of it.

Yet the question is a live one. I wrestled with it some years ago while watching two television programs. I had switched on the set, hoping to kill some time in a rather lonely setting in eastern Illinois. The TV, an ancient one, finally warmed to the occasion, and into view came a somewhat stiffly choreographed gaggle of young people singing the latest "with-it" religious tune. Then from the midst emerged a tall figure, handsomely dressed, who pointed his finger at me and announced, "Something *good* is going to happen to you!" His prophecy was fulfilled thirty seconds later when, on another channel, I viewed a remarkable CBS documentary on the amazing Brazilian archbishop, Dom Helder Camara.

Now both these men are called evangelicals, both represent discernible life-styles consistent with their understanding of the gospel. Both accept Jesus Christ as the norm for discipleship. One reflects the affluence and influence of North American evangelicalism, the other the hard life of the peasantry and the oppressed.

I was fascinated, because I knew that here were two different perceptions of what it means to be evangelical. Here were almost certainly two different views of what salvation means to the marginal masses in our century. Here were two men who, in their struggle to follow Christ, personalize a central issue among believers in the world today: not so much the question of evangelical identity, but more crucially, the question of salvation in our times. What does salvation mean in the age of Big Brother? Or to put the same question another way, what is the gospel? How can it be perceived as good news by our fellowmen?

We raise this question here because we are concerned about the present and the future. Hence, we have chosen not to dwell on the past. This is unfortunate in a way, but it makes my task easier. I am not an historian. But I have asked other men who are about the history of evangelical social concern. They refer me to Timothy Smith, or to Alan Heimert or Perry Miller, perhaps Kenneth Scott Latourette. I've read Mr. Henry's *Uneasy Conscience* and Mr. Wirt's *Social Conscience*. I've attended what evangelical leaders call "historic" conferences where attempts were made to "speak to the issues." I was in Berlin, Minneapolis, Cincinnati, Dallas—I'm a professional conference-goer. I was also invited to share in the conference on salvation today, sponsored by the World Council of Churches in Bangkok.

Why all this research? Because I needed some evidence that this thing called Christianity as viewed by us evangelicals has made a difference in the lives of the oppressed of the world. Black students wanted that information—they have heard our spokesmen, visited our churches, interpreted our guilty silence in the face of monstrous social outrages, and have concluded that social concern and evangelicals were mutually incompatible. There is very little evidence over the past hundred years to disprove that conclusion.

Sadly, there is very little evidence currently to disprove it either. With one possible exception: Some years ago Harry Golden spoke of a phenomenon in the South which he claimed was unique in our country's history . . . the emergence of a different revolutionary, the black man. Golden identified two weapons used by black men to force communication and recognition. "One is the writ, the brief, the court argument . . . the law, the oldest complex in our Anglo-Saxon civilization. The second weapon is even more remarkable. It is Christianity, the oldest complex in our Western civilization."[1]

This celebrated author, editor of the *Carolina Israelite,* also spoke about evangelicals. He said,

The evangelical plantation owner saw no relationship between religion and politics. He forgot that

---

1. *Mr. Kennedy and the Negroes* (New York: Crest) p. 16.

while Christianity is a group effort to realize the joys of an afterlife, that effort is realized only through an individual ethic here and now—little did the Southerner suspect that one day the descendants of slaves would wield Christianity as a finely tooled political weapon, asking jobs, schools, wages, and hospitals in its name.[2]

He concluded, "If Christianity is saving the Negro, so is he saving Christianity."[3] Interesting insight. And yet evangelicals were conspicuous by their absence in that struggle precisely because they did not perceive it as being evangelical.

The inadequacy examined. Why? In the first place, we seem to have an inadequate theology of sin. We have dwelled so long on the gross sins of individuals that we have very little understanding of the corporate nature of sin. We can only speak meaningfully of evangelical social concern if we understand the relationship between individual sin and its corporate consequences. Rosemary Reuther is helpful when she writes,

Even in Saint Paul, the personal movement of conversion and reconciliation with God cannot be separated from his gathering into the community of reconciliation and promise, for these are two sides of one and the same thing. By the same token it is

---

2. Ibid., pp. 16,17.
3. Ibid., p. 17.

clear that, for Paul, the state of sin, alienation, and brokenness between man and God does not result simply in individual "bad acts" but stands within a corporate structure of alienation and oppression which has raised up a social and cosmic "anti-creation." The individualistic concept of sin ignores this social-cosmic dimension of evil.[4]

She continues:

A prophetic sense of sin might indeed acknowledge that sin begins in the personal ("cor curvum in se") but its expression is corporate, social, and even cosmic. Sin builds up a corporate structure of alienation and oppression which man, individually, cannot overcome. This corporate structure of sin distorts the character of man in community and in creation so fundamentally that it can be visualized as a false world.[5]

Now we evangelicals know this. We teach this in the schools we sponsor. The people who write our journals know this. But this reality is treated as an abstraction. Sin is real, but slums are not; we have not shown the ethical and moral connection between sin and slums. Greed is real, but excessive profiteering in the name of free enterprise is not; lust is real, but we prefer to inveigh against the swivel-hipped secretary who ambles seductively down the office aisle rather than the callous

---

4. *Liberation Theology* (New York: Paulist) p. 8.
5. Ibid.

manipulation of the Justice Department to reelect a President.

We fail to acknowledge that as members of the community of fallen men, we are responsible for the misery of others; we have not only practiced sin, but have also rejoiced with others who did likewise. The fruit of that corporate sin now provides the economic base for our evangelical institutions.

Secondly, we have preached, and do preach a privatistic application of the Cross, which is inadequate. The Cross, in the minds of most American Christians, is either an historical artifact upon which Jesus died or else a bad case of lumbago. But in the experience of our Lord, it was "the judgment of this world" (John 12:31). We have called men to repent on issues that God is not the least bit concerned about. Rather, conversion requires a proclamation of the Cross that awakens the individual to his need for a radical change. The individual must be confronted by a demand that illumines not only his responsibility for his own sin, but also his culpability for the creation and perpetuation of society's corporate sins. Thus is created a new person, one who repents of his involvement in the world, his mental surrender to the group-think of Big Brother; a person who renounces his advantages in the present order to assume a place among the wretched of the earth.

Lesslie Newbigin put it so well:

Our faith is that the Word of the Cross is in very truth the power of God unto salvation—not just the rescue of each one of us separately, but the healing, the making whole of the whole creation and the fulfilling of God's whole will. Our faith is that the Cross is in truth the only event in human history which can properly be called the crisis of human history, and that the issue which is raised there for the entire human race is one beside which even the survival of human civilization on earth is a secondary matter.[6]

Thirdly, we suffer from what Helmut Thielicke calls a "false conservatism"—an attitude which fails to perceive the political implications of the Church's prophetic and pastoral role in society. Says Thielicke:

False conservatism expresses itself in the inclination to accept world conditions as they are. Under this pseudoconservative banner, a corrupt social order, which keeps part of humanity living at substandard economic levels while allowing another class to exploit and profiteer, is regarded as a matter of divine providence—or visitation—calling for simple acceptance and submission .... To refer the existing social and political situation directly to divine providence, and to ignore the secondary human causes—the guilt and error of individuals and of organized groups—is to create among Christians a condition which we might describe as political apathy. If everything that takes place is regarded as

---

6. *Bible Society Record* (February, 1961) p. 19.

God's doing, then it is obviously sanctioned by what is assumed to be the will of God. Logically, then, it can never be opposed. Even though child labor, malnutrition, and the oppression and humiliation of millions cry out to heaven, they must simply be accepted.

It is a terrible judgment on Christianity and on false theology that the decisive social movements of the last hundred years have not originated in any will on the part of the Church to play the good Samaritan. The Church has not taken the Lord's command to "love thy neighbor" as a concrete commission to change a blatantly unjust social situation. No, the decisive impulses for change have come from within the ranks of the oppressed and humiliated themselves. There has thus been nourished a kind of revolutionary instinct, the terrible symptoms of which may now be seen throughout the world, in their extreme form in communism . . . . To be sure, Christians have helped the needy. Think of the Church's many works of mercy and of the countless acts of private charity. But these were bound to be regarded as alms, and hence as humiliating to the recipients, a cover-up for the unjust situation, so long as the proletariat was given the impression that the Church actually tolerated the unjust situation as a whole—and did so in the name of that evil conservatism which even dared to claim sanction for itself in the will of God.[7]

It seems obvious that the fault of much that parades as evangelical is far more American than

---

7. *Political Ethics* (Philadelphia: Fortress, 1969) 11: 627, 628.

Christian in its attitudes and stance toward the oppressed among us. We don't particularly care for the poor in our own ranks, and technology and affluence have made it possible for us to avoid them. Technology has produced the freeways, and affluence (with the complicity of the Federal Housing Authority) has produced the suburbs.

But what about the future? The question is not whether the evangelical has a future. Given the self-perpetuating nature of institutions, it is probable that we shall see most of our organizations prosper "till Jesus comes." Beyond that, the ball gets cloudy. The question is rather: Is there any future for evangelicals in social action?

There is, of course, and there is now a mood among a new breed of evangelicals which can make significant breakthroughs. Some of this new leadership had its sensitivities honed to razor edge in the sixties as part of the student protest movements. What many older evangelicals do not admit is that much of the current aggravation about social concerns owes its life to these and other civil-rights movements. Now older, and recovering from the shock induced by the collapse of the New Left, many of these people are also discovering in the New Testament a more radical discipleship than their fathers knew. Some of these people have made their way into evangelical seminaries and will be exerting significant leadership in the near future.

But there is also a discernible pulse among older leaders also. What I have called the "Mood of Minneapolis" is still haunting many of those gathered for that occasion. The response to the ministries of Tom Skinner, Keith Miller, Leighton Ford, and others who advocated strong social commitments was heartening, and these delegates could provide the basis of new coalitions for social action as well as a means to bridge some serious gaps in communication between generations.

To complement this evangelical mood is a profoundly significant change of attitude in America, particularly in intellectual circles. Robert Heilbroner puts it like this:

We are experiencing the onset of a new mood in the seventies. This new mood is conservative, although not in the usual sense in which the word is used in political debate. I would describe it as the rediscovery of a perspective on human events that highlights certain aspects of history, of "human nature," if I may risk the term to which both the liberal mood of the fifties and the radical mood of the sixties paid insufficient attention, if in fact they paid it any attention at all . . . .

[This new mood] dwells on the persistence of human folly in the face of heroic efforts to enlighten it with reason; on the perversity and cruelty that provide an insistent *basso ostinato* to the melodies of progress; on the extraordinary ease with which human sacrifice can be marshaled for war and the tremendous difficulties of adducing it for the tasks of peace; on the susceptibility of men and women at all levels of society to the delusions of nationalism or organized religion and their virtual immunity from any sense of human "brotherhood" with men and women of another territory or faith.[8]

Heilbroner calls this mood "radical conservatism" and cites as one of its key features its willingness to ask terrible questions "that go to the root of things."

Why does mankind refuse to make the changes, often within easy grasp, that might rid it of the oppression which it has known from earliest times? Why do human beings display the laziness, the cowardice, the stupidity, inertia, or indifference that allows things to go on as they are?[9]

These will be acknowledged by evangelicals as root questions, and if Heilbroner is correct, then it is possible to take advantage of this conservative frame of mind. The Scriptures supply the answer to this moral and ethical dilemma of man. But the evangelical church will need to overcome serious deficiencies in order to seize the moment for God. While in the forefront in the proclamation of the Scripture's answer to man's moral dilemma, the evangelical has been deficient in his understanding of the way in which man frames his current crises. The late Abraham Joshua Heschel

---

8. *The New York Review* (October 15, 1972).

9. Ibid.

exhibits a profound insight at this point:

> The most serious obstacle which modern men encounter in entering a discussion about the ideas of the Bible is the absence of the problem to which the Bible refers. This, indeed, is the status of the Bible in modern society: it is a sublime answer, but we no longer know the question to which it responds. Unless we recover the question, there is no hope of understanding the Bible.[10]

Another voice is that of Rollo May, famed psychotherapist. In a critique of a major premise of much of the literature promising a new age, Dr. May declares, "Far from Consciousness III being an answer, it would be no consciousness at all, for it lacks the dialectic movement between yes and no, good and evil, which gives birth to consciousness of any sort."[11] Commenting on Charles Reich's contention that a new order will come because there are no enemies out there, May queries,

> Are there no enemies? Can we call to mind the Berrigan brothers and think that? Or the Soledad brothers? Or Angela Davis? Or the convicts at Attica, who after the slaughter were forced to run the gauntlet naked? Or Vietnam? Reich has no understanding of the creeping fascism already

---

10. Cited in *The Center Magazine* (Santa Barbara, Calif.: The Fund for the Republic), March/April, 1973, p.43.

11. *Power and Innocence: A Search for the Sources of Violence* (New York: Norton, 1972) p. 54.

discernible in our country: the turning of youth against their fathers, the anti-intellectualism, the growth of violence coupled with the sense of powerlessness of the mass of people, the tendencies of bureaucracies to make decisions on the basis of what works mechanically with all human sense drowned in opportunism.[12]

There are many other voices, and a cursory examination of bookstalls would reveal the intensity of concern. By and large, the evangelical church is not tuned to the sounds of the seventies, and this inadequacy must be corrected.

A further task for the evangelical church is to disengage herself from her captivity to cultural conservatism of the sort described by Thielicke. Only then can she speak to the moral issues that threaten the very survival of a free society; only then can she become a true servanthood in the world.

---

12. Ibid., p. 55.

2

Engagement—
the Christian's Agenda

Foy Valentine

The prophet Joel said, "Your old men shall dream dreams, your young men shall see visions" (2:28). As a middle-aged man of fifty, neither old so as to dream dreams nor young so as to see visions, what shall I say? Perhaps I may be permitted, among friends, to speak of actualizing dreams and realizing visions, to address myself to our agenda of engagement, for "we have promises to keep, and miles to go before we sleep."

Obviously I am biting off more than I can chew. It would be impossible to do justice to the points I

Foy Valentine has been executive secretary of the Southern Baptist Convention's Christian Life Commission since 1960. He is a graduate of Baylor (B.A., 1944) and Southwestern Baptist Theological Seminary (Th. M., 1947; Th.D., 1949) and pastored several churches in Texas. He is the author of four books and the compiler of two others; two of his sermons have appeared in Best Sermons.

want to make even if I were writing a book, and a long one at that.

For Christian prophets from the beginning there have been many struggles, many conflicts, many battles, many confrontations. These are never won. Not really. For evangelicals committed to Christian social concern and Christian social action, I reckon they are not even supposed to be. We live with the conviction that God has put fire in our bones and given us the stomach for the battle. If we couldn't stand the heat, we wouldn't stay in the kitchen. Our agenda is engagement. And in this agenda, "It is required in stewards, that a man be found faithful" (I Corinthians 4:2).

Let us then, brothers and sisters, consider our calling.

Who we are. Really, now, who are we evangelicals interested in Christian social concern?

We are God's. Jesus loves us; this we know, for the Bible tells us so; and an amazing number of fellow Christians tell us so too. We are God's people through Jesus Christ. We are not interested in becoming Unitarians and in singing hymns to race relations, sewage disposal, and sex education. We are just interested in being God's people and in doing his thing. Sometimes we have headed for Spain but God has stopped us off in Rome. We have sought to preach the gospel of

God in Christ, but have sometimes had to "fight with beasts at Ephesus" (I Corinthians 15:32). We have undertaken an emphasis on Christian morality, but our lot has been to deal with misunderstanding among our own brethren.

So be it. We are not mad at anybody. We are especially not mad at God. And God is not mad at us. In the Rome where we find ourselves now, we find sufficient strength in the overwhelming conviction that we are God's. Thank God! We remember that, despondent, Tchaikovsky waded into the ice-filled Moskva River, hoping for disaster to follow, but that providence chose for him to survive to write his last three symphonies.

We are evangelical Christians. We are sometimes forced to do battle with other evangelical Christians. Within our own fellowships there are treasons which must be challenged. We can announce God's judgments on these treasons only from within. For our kind to withdraw from our respective conventions or to renounce the reality of our Christian heritage and the specificity of our peculiar calling would be even less intelligent than if we were to take our own lives. So, we are neither inordinately proud nor especially ashamed that we are evangelical Christians. This is just who we are.

We are ordained. We understand ourselves to be ordered, elected, set apart. We are ministers, literally and excitingly—prophetic ministers brought, we firmly believe, to the Kingdom for such a time as this. We believe our Christian faith has profound social consequences and we are "ordained a lamp" for God's people (Psalm 132:17). We are ordered to carry this torch. We would joust with no windmills, but in a real, not imagined moral solvency, we would lead evangelicals to apply Christian principles in every area and relationship of life. Our ordainment, we fully understand, is not to polarize. God, it seems to me, always attends to that. The Bible knows a lot about polarization: sheep and goats, wheat and chaff, wise and foolish, saved and damned, good and evil, heaven and hell, life and death. Polarization is at the heart of reality. It is not in and of itself evil. We view our ordainment, our election, as an easy yoke, a light burden, a chosen cross which we bear not only resolutely but also joyously for Christ's sake.

We are sinners. We are not just honorary sinners. We are real sinners. We understand not only that our churches are running a fever but also that we ourselves run a fever as well. There are serpents in *our* garden, and too often we heed their counsel. There are extremely important marks for us to hit, and too frequently we miss those marks, more grievously, I fear, by omission than by commission. There is a world of good to do; and too often we do it not. Social concern among evangelicals has *not* come of age and we know this full well. We are remembering daily Paul's admonition, "Let him that thinketh he standeth take heed lest he fall" (I Corinthians 10:12) and are trying hard not to be like the poor piano player who practices his mistakes.

We are pilgrims. We are an Exodus people. We count not ourselves to have apprehended (Philippians 3:13); we seek a city whose builder and maker is God (Hebrews 11:10). We believe that the way of Jesus Christ our Lord is an applied way, a living way, a way of *aggiornamento*—moving toward the day. We believe, to paraphrase Toynbee's observation about civilization, that Christianity is a movement and not a condition, a voyage and not a harbor. We are a part of God's pilgrim people, his movement, his kind of folks. We seek a better world. Our horse must stay always saddled; our motor must be always running; we must be always leaving on some jet plane.

What we are doing. Evangelicals working in Christian social concern are seeking to help our churches to effect social change for God's glory and man's good.

Change may very well be the word our age knows best. To cite Alvin Toffler's *Future Shock,* we are "overwhelmed by change," experiencing "the dizzying disorientation brought on by the premature arrival of the future."[1] The task is formidable. Many Christians are becoming angry at those within the churches who agitate for action and press for social change. These believe there is

---

1. (New York: Bantam, 1971) pp. 1, 11.

no place in the Church for social concern. They want the Bible preached in the truncated form to which they have become accustomed in the culture religion of our established churches. They would abolish our work and obliterate our emphasis from the Church's life. They view us as a vermiform appendix in the Church's body politic and insist that it would be a great service to God and to the Church to rid the body of the obnoxious organ. In the most social era of man's history they are obsessed with the radical individualism that in some measure is harbored in the heart of every one of us. That rugged individualism which has made evangelicals strong may, in today's world, now prevent our claiming our share of the future—what has pushed us forward may now hold us back. These radical individualists view religion as purely personal and the Church's task as that of providing preaching, Bible study, and a soul-saving service. They hold that on their own initiative saved souls may then find whatever avenues they can to do what God may want done in the world.

Our task is to convert these *modernists,* who have turned away from Moses and the prophets and Paul and John and Peter and James and from Jesus to embrace that wretchedly false and abominably misleading dualism which never ceases to plague the Christian church.

Our task is to convince our alienated brethren who seek to turn the Church away from the great issues of our time that if, indeed, we did turn away, the world would be impoverished and the Church's whole life and work would be invalidated. For if God's people cannot confront the issues that affect the lives of mankind with the reconciling gospel of Christ in such a way as to convince unbelievers, then evangelism is empty and missions is mockery.

Our task is to hold the young, the educated, the active, and the committed who have about given up on the Church and to convince them that integrity requires them to stay in the Church, to support the Church, to give to the Church, and to be the Church.

Our task is to help Christian leaders at every level of church life to understand that God's basic concern is not religion but life and to see that there can be no turning back from responsible involvement in the world and responsible commitment to effect social change for God's glory and man's good. A continued rejection of social fads, unbaptized humanism, unbiblical pietism, and moral posturing—yes. But disengagement—no. Uninvolvement in this age is not a live option for the people of God. Our task is to help Christians to understand that sin is both personal and social and that we cannot be true to God and wink at the great social sins of ecological rape, militarism, white racism, sexism, poverty in the midst of plenty, crime, consumer exploitation by business, inflation, unemployment, overpopulation, and the like.

In the escalating battle for the soul of the

Church between those who in the name of Christ and purely personal religion would retreat from the issues and those who in the name of Christ and his full gospel with its social imperative seek to confront and solve the issues, our task is to help evangelicals save their souls and do the work of God regarding social change.

Contrary to what today's humanistic activists are saying, Christ cannot be Lord without also being Savior. And contrary to what today's pietistic fundamentalists are saying, Christ cannot be Savior without also being Lord. Our task is to help evangelicals see that withdrawal and involvement, conservatism and radicalism, worship and work, reflection and action, practicing and preaching, the personal and the social—these all must be everlastingly linked in the life and work of the Church, or else the Church goes off into grievous and inexcusable heresy.

Theological presuppositions for our agenda of involvement. I suggest three theological presuppositions for effecting social change: Things need changing; Christians are obligated to change them; and God's people can do it.

(1) Things need changing. The given of our world is that man is degenerate; our communities are corrupt; the race is fallen; society is sick; the world is not as it ought to be; things need changing. Let us not always decry change, running through the streets like Chicken Little, crying that the sky is falling when an acorn drops, go-

ing about wringing our hands and looking back longingly like Lot's wife, speaking and acting in direct contradiction to the Bible's clear injunction, "Say not, 'Why were the former days better than these?' For it is not from wisdom that you ask this" (Ecclesiastes 7:10, RSV). Multitudes regularly make their beds in hell. War is a kind of hell. Poverty is a kind of hell. Pollution is a kind of hell. Overpopulation is a kind of hell. Overcrowding is a kind of hell. Loneliness is a kind of hell. Rats are a kind of hell. Flies are a kind of hell. Worms are a kind of hell. Sickness is a kind of hell. Hate is a kind of hell. Despair is a kind of hell. Crime is a kind of hell. Alcohol precipitates a kind of hell. Drugs introduce a kind of hell. Oppression is a kind of hell. Injustice is a kind of hell. Unemployment is a kind of hell. Inflation is a kind of hell. Insanity is a kind of hell. Prisons are a kind of hell.

Today's world in which Christians are called to a responsible use of church power is a strange, disfigured, hurting world. Man is a sinner. And our institutions are massively infected with sin. Almost by definition, institutions resist social change, culture resists criticism, the organized church cultivates conformity. But things need changing.

(2) The divine imperative: Christians are obligated to change things. Involvement is the corollary of incarnation for God. Albert Camus' main character in *The Fall,* Jean-Baptiste Clamence, takes his leave of the chance acquain-

tance with whom he has been walking in the Amsterdam night, saying:

> ... No, you will easily find your way now: I'll leave you near this bridge at night. It's the result of a vow. Suppose, after all, that someone should jump in the water. One of two things—either you do likewise to fish him out and, in cold weather, you run a great risk! Or you forsake him there and suppressed dives sometimes leave one strangely aching. Good-night.[2]

It is just such disengagement and uninvolvement which today has left the Church strangely aching.

In *The Divine Imperative,* subtitled "A Protestant Ethic," Emil Brunner wrote in 1936, *"What ought we to do,* is the great question of humanity. It is the entrance to the Christian Faith; none can evade it who wish[es] to enter the sanctuary. But it is also the gate through which one passes out of the sanctuary again, back into life." We properly concern ourselves with the question "What ought we to do?" to effect social change.

The Bible's teachings concerning this divine imperative to change the world are clear.

"Do justly, love mercy, and walk humbly with thy God."

"Cease to do evil, learn to do good."

"Let justice roll down as waters, and righteousness . . . ."

"Seek peace and pursue it . . . ."

---

2. (New York: Vintage, 1956) pp. 6,7.

"Follow after righteousness . . . ."

"Pure religion and undefiled before God is this . . . ."

"Faith without works is dead . . . ."

"Thy kingdom come. Thy will be done in earth . . . ."

"Thou shalt love the Lord . . . and thy neighbor . . . ."

(3) We have it in us, by God's grace, to do better: we can effect social change. Many today are so hostile to the central institutions of society that they never abandon their posture of alienation; but Christians know a more excellent way, a way of reconciliation, a way of renewal, a way of redemption, a way of right relationships. God has something better for the world. Through the Church, spiritual Israel, shall all the nations of the earth yet be blessed. With eyes of faith we see renewal for "whosoever will." With eyes of hope we see renewal for society in general, our communities in particular. With eyes of love we see renewal for the world.

Goals of social change.

(1) Righteousness. This is one of the profoundest concepts in the Bible. The Kingdom of God is the Kingdom of right relations. Order and right relations among people are overwhelmingly important to the health of society, and Christians concerned about social changes are necessarily concerned about righteousness.

(2) Justice. Nothing so upsets us as injustice. Is

not this a universal phenomenon? Moses killed the Egyptian because of an overwhelming sense of injustice that drove him to a shameful act of passion. The American Revolution began over an infinitesimal tax on tea as the colonists became incensed over the injustice of taxation without representation. Justice simply has to be a major target for Christians concerned about social action.

(3) Freedom. It is not in dramatic acts but in small failures that freedom's light burns out. As Christians we cannot believe with Marx that man is economically determined, or with Freud that he is sexually determined, or with Dewey that he is educationally determined, or with modern social planners that he is socially determined, or with B.F. Skinner that he is environmentally determined. Man is meant to be free. God means for all men to know the truth and to be made free by the truth. Some who profess commitment to the great Baptist heritage of freedom are now eagerly reaching out a misguided hand to steady a tottering ark and keep the truth safe. What a travesty! God, who alone is free, will not suffer his truth to fall or to fail. My Christian freedom is a corollary of God's freedom. Freedom for mankind is our ideal and another of our targets for action.

(4) Peace. No scene in the life of Christ is packed with more pathos than where Jesus stands weeping over Jerusalem and cries, "Would that even today you knew the things that make for peace!" (Luke 19:42, RSV). In Jesus Christ, God

has shown himself to be not merely a peace lover staying at home out of trouble, hoping to avoid conflict with the staus quo; but being a peacemaker, he stirred things up like crazy, living his life in a running battle with the establishment until his enemies finally nailed him. Our commitment to work for the things that make for peace must be a strong and disciplined and continuing commitment, for peace is one of the most important goals of social change.

(5) The good life: health, fulfillment, education, service, the abundant life are all qualities which the Christian not only seeks for himself but also seeks to establish in the community.

Effecting social change. "Thy kingdom come. Thy will be done in earth, as it is in heaven" (Matthew 6:10). Christians universally pray this prayer which the Lord taught his disciples to pray. The Kingdom ought to come; it needs to come; we want it to come; man's highest hope is that it will come. But how? *How shall we implement that prayer? How* shall we change the world? *What methods* shall we use in our ministry of renewal and reconciliation?

In Christian social concern, we could easily be preoccupied with such vital concerns as the *theology* and *goals* of social change to the complete neglect of methods. It would be possible, of course, to turn our attention too exclusively to methods while neglecting theology and goals. Our more common failure as evangelical Christians today, however, may very well be our failure to develop and exercise those methods of social change which will enable us actually to *be* God's reconciling agents in what Tennessee Williams has called "a world lit by lightning."

There is danger in methods. They are utterly inadequate as gods; but they are absolutely indispensable as tools in service for God. Without valid methods for social change, any group is compelled to start all over again with every generation in any worthy undertaking for social change, not learning from God's revelation, from his dealings with others in days gone by, or from the Church's past experience. Without biblically validated, authentically Christian methods, our evangelical cause will remain essentially immobilized in the vast arena of social change; and it is on this arena where the eyes of modern man are now focused.

Karl Marx, in his thesis on Feuerbach, observed that while philosophers have explained the world, his commitment was to change the world. We do find it easy to describe the world but hard to change it. It is easy to diagnose the world's ills but hard to cure them. It is easy to resolve about the world's problems but hard actually to resolve them. It is easy to reflect on social change but inordinately hard to effect it.

Christians are in the world-changing business. We believe that "God so loved the world, that he gave his only begotten Son, that whosoever

70

believeth in him should not perish, but have everlasting life" (John 3:16). This is our task: *to change men* for God and for good, *to change economic systems* for God and for good, *to change the structures of society* for God and for good, *to change the world* for God and for good—this is our task, and this is our high calling in Christ Jesus. Our business is to "turn the world upside down" (Acts 17:6) for God, extending God's Kingdom until "the kingdoms of this world are become the kingdoms of our Lord, and of his Christ" (Revelation 11:15).

At various times and in different circumstances many methods of social change have been employed by Christians. This occasion allows for no definitive statement concerning methods of social change; but two primary methods commend themselves to Christians everywhere and at all times: first, regeneration/transformation, and second, penetration/permeation. A third method, organization, commends itself especially to Christians today.

(1) Regeneration and transformation. Social change for Christians is in some real sense wrapped up in regeneration, and regeneration is the grace of God apprehended through repentance and faith. True Christian repentance and true Christian faith are, at once, the *genesis,* the *environment,* the *habitat,* the *method,* and the *goal* of the social change for which Christians work and pray.

Repentance is the keynote of the New Testament. It is a complete change of mental outlook, life design, and social relationships. It is not to try harder but rather to accept God's way of looking at things and working in the world. Its social consequences are gloriously attested to in the Bible and throughout history. Without repentance, a stuttering, stumbling, stalling Church would remain forever powerless to cast out the devils of racism, sexism, war, poverty, exploitation, injustice, pollution, overpopulation, and all the other evils that dog the feet of mankind.

Faith, for the Christian, is standing always at attention in the presence of God to say, "Lord, what would you have me to do?" Faith is the apprehension of "the power to become." As faith's revolutionary power lays hold of God's grace to change believers, so faith's revolutionary power lays hold of God's grace to change the world.

Regeneration, God's work of grace, apprehended through repentance and faith, is both personal and social, for God's Word is not, and will not be, bound.

It is important to bear in mind that there are both socially conservative and socially radical dimensions in Christian regeneration. Both dimensions are necessary if Christians are to avoid social anarchy on the one hand and social stagnation on the other.

For Christians, social change is rightly brought about through love and self-sacrifice, characterized by the principle of the Cross. The task of changing attitudes in regeneration and transformation is a task for which the people of God are uniquely, peculiarly qualified. Anytime we go beyond a concern for pointing men to the Lamb of God who takes away the sin of the world, we go beyond God.

(2) Penetration and permeation. The early Christians made great headway against overwhelming odds because they confronted the world not with an aggressive program of direct social reform or a superior system of speculative philosophy but with a consistently and uniformly better way of life—better family life, better community life, better business life, better human relations, better citizenship, better social life, and better moral life. In the early church, ordinary men and women were motivated by the Lord Christ to change the world. Their primary method was one of penetration and permeation in a spirit of self-giving love, bearing in mind *whose* they were and *who* they were.

Under God, they understood themselves to be *salt* ("Ye are the salt of the earth," Jesus said in Matthew 5:13), *light* ("Ye are the light of the world," Jesus said in Matthew 5:14), *seed* ("Unto what is the kingdom of God like? . . . It is like a grain of mustard seed, which a man took, and cast into his garden; and it grew, and waxed a great tree . . .," Jesus said in Luke 13:18,19), and *leaven* ("Whereunto shall I liken the kingdom of God? It is like leaven, which a woman took and hid in three measures of meal, till the whole was leavened," Jesus said in Luke 13:20,21).

How far into the world shall Christians penetrate? *How much* of society shall we permeate? How many knees shall bow? God puts absolutely no limit on Christians in our ministry of penetration and permeation. The field is the world.

(3) Organization. As it is the Christian thing to do to bind up the wounds and pay the hospital bills for a man who has fallen among thieves on a Jericho road, so it is the Christian thing to do to organize and act to effect social change. Culbert G. Rutenber has spoken discerningly to this point:

> Suppose the Good Samaritan, later, had formed a committee—The Committee for Making the Jericho Road a Safe Highway. Suppose the committee had put on a big publicity campaign and and forced City Hall to string lights along the Jericho Road, to remove the shrubbery in which the thieves were accustomed to hide before pouncing, and to increase the number of policemen who patrolled the road? Why . . . would not this too be a form of neighbor love? And if City Hall refused because it was in cahoots with the thieves, who regularly "paid off" the politicians, would it not be an act of kindness to all potential future victims for the committee to agitate for the removal of the grafters in the next election and the installation of an administration which would do these things? If the motive were the same—for the love of Christ and the neighbor—would not this, too, be a form of Christian good deeds? True,

this involves corporate action rather than individual action and therefore is a kind of love-at-a-distance (as someone has defined justice), being more indirect. But what of that? How many kinds of good works are exempted from the injunction to perform "all good works"?[3]

By virtue of our current Christian strength in numbers, money, power, and influence, evangelicals have responsibilities to society which are proportionately much greater than those incumbent on the early Christians. God has given much to us; and of us shall much be required.

How is Christ incarnate today? Where is the Church? How are we to help evangelical Christians to be the Church in today's world?

Believing that the revealed religion of the Bible requires the correlation of religion and life, we insist on confronting the world with the gospel. This technique is itself a kind of action.

We must speak directly and critically, prophetically and reconcilingly to social issues, for the pretense of neutrality is even more transparent in our day than it was in Pilate's day. It is the eternal relevance of Christ Jesus our Lord, God's Living Word, who has prevented Christianity from following Zoroastrianism and Shintoism into the oblivion reserved for religions that have no word from the Lord for their cultures. We

---

3. *The Reconciling Gospel* (Nashville: Broadman, 1969) pp. 101, 102.

must conduct conferences, organize committees, enlist workers, exercise power, and do the work, carrying the good news of God in Christ out into every area and relationship of life.

Conclusion. In this emphasis on Christian social concern, I am not calling for a newly militant Church to place itself at the disposition of every new humanitarian venture, seeking social change just for the sake of change. I am rather calling for Christians newly infused with commitment to Christ's ministry of reconciliation to bring his specifically Christian, specifically redemptive, specifically reconciling good news to all men, to all our communities, and to all the world.

I am calling for changed men to change the world.

Malcolm Muggeridge has told of an old missionary he came across while living in South India.

This good man had got in the way of appearing each year at a local Hindu festival and denouncing the god Shiva, before whom devotees were prostrating themselves. At first he was stoned, then just cursed and insulted, and finally taken for granted. When the time came for him to retire, the organizers of the festival petitioned his missionary society to send a replacement. He had become part of the show.[4]

---

4. "The Decade of the Great Liberal Death Wish," *Esquire* (December, 1970) p. 155.

It is our hope that Christian evangelicals will not become just a part of the show. It is rather our hope, our prayer, and our purpose to help the Church to move forward for God and for good with our agenda—engagement.

3

Prayer and Social Concern

Paul S. Rees

Let me begin with an echo from a voice that a few weeks ago was stilled by death. Some twenty-five years ago Dr. Albert E. Day wrote a thoughtful, confessional, stimulating book to which he gave the title *An Autobiography of Prayer.* From it I quote:

This can be said without presumption—that one who truly prays will have keener insight, will form

Paul S. Rees is a veteran churchman who has served as vice-president at large of World Vision International since 1958. Prior to that, he was pastor of Minneapolis' First Covenant Church for twenty years. A 1923 graduate of the University of Southern California, he has been awarded five honorary doctorates over the years, has written 14 books and numerous articles, and has spoken in more than 60 countries.

sounder judgment, will evolve more intelligent plans, will achieve a greater mastery of situations, will sustain more creative relationships with people than he ever would without prayer.[1]

Alongside that sentence let me lay the witness of a better-known Christian whose notable exterior deeds were the fine fruit of his interior devotion. I refer to the late Frank Laubach. In one of his earliest books he tells about a day spent alone with God on a hilltop in the Philippine Islands. Feeling himself a futile, frustrated missionary, he that day was caught up into the life of the Spirit. The meaning of openness to the Spirit broke over him in a way that he had not known in all his previous Christian experience.

After referring to the sort of commitment he made to God for a life of prayer, he goes on to say: "And I added another resolve—to be as wide open towards people and their need as I am towards God. Windows open *outward* as well as upward."[2]

It is this second dimension of prayer—windows opening *outward* as well as upward—that engages us now.

Prayer as *escape* must first be faced.

In reality it is not the God-dimension of

---

1. (New York: Harper and Brothers, 1952) p. 146.

2. *Letters by a Modern Mystic* (New York: Student Volunteer Movement, 1937) p. 9.

prayer that endangers or precludes the people-dimension. The peril must be located elsewhere, namely, in the sphere of verbalization. George Meredith, the novelist, once defined sentimentalism as "enjoyment without obligation." We sentimentalize prayer too easily. Enamored by the forms and phrases of prayer, we mistake a shallow emotion for an authentic confrontation. Thus prayer becomes escape, not spur.

Nowhere in Holy Scripture is this peril faced more starkly or denounced more unsparingly than in the prophets. Recall how the book of Isaiah begins. Here are some soundings in a devastating indictment:

"What to me is the multitude of your sacrifices?" (v. 11)[3]

"When you come to appear before me, who requires of you this trampling of my courts?" (v. 12)

"When you spread forth your hands, I will hide my eyes from you; even though you make many prayers, I will not listen; your hands are full of blood" (v. 15).

Then, with equally trenchant positiveness, this:

"Cease to do evil, learn to do good; seek justice, correct oppression; defend the fatherless, plead for the widow" (vs. 16,17).

It was Isaiah's unpopular role to tell Jerusalem and Judah that at one and the same time a society can be sinfully sick and sentimentally religious.

---

3. Biblical quotations in this chapter are from the Revised Standard Version.

Until both personal and corporate responsibility are faced, God will continue to say, "Even though you make many prayers, I will not listen."

Prayer as escape from social concern and initiative—this is what has emerged too often in history for us to be unaware of its danger in ourselves today.

Moving to ground that is less negative, let's try to say something relevant about prayer as *empathy*.

If empathy is a fusion of imagination, perception, and emotion, a kind of creative concern that enables us, in some very real sense, to put ourselves in the place of others, then one of the values of prayer, if it be more than a verbal anesthetic, is that it gives the Spirit of God a chance to enliven our imagination, to sharpen our perception, and to deepen our emotion.

We do well to remind ourselves of the broad range of concerns that Jesus had for people in their varied situations of need. In a Matthew account we are told that "Jesus went about all the cities and villages, teaching in their synagogues and preaching the gospel of the kingdom, and healing every disease and every infirmity" (9:35).

If that was his ministry, what was its motivation? Matthew gives the answer: "When he saw the crowds, he had compassion for them, because they were harassed and helpless, like sheep without a shepherd" (v. 36). His perceptivity was linked with his empathy, and out from that combination of motivating factors flowed his ministry.

Now I am bound to believe that when this portrait of the empathetic Christ is joined with a summons to prayer, as it is by Matthew, something more is involved than sheer coincidence or pious tradition. "Then he said to his disciples, 'The harvest is plentiful, but the laborers are few; pray therefore the Lord of the harvest to send out laborers into his harvest'" (v. 37). Let there be an exercise of prayer whose focus and fruit will be the emergence of Kingdom workers who will demonstrably share their Master's perceptivity and empathy and thus their Master's activity as well.

Archie Hargraves, as part of the invocation at a large synodical gathering of churchmen, once prayed:

> O God, who lives in tenements, goes to segregated schools, is beaten in precincts, is unemployed, help us to know you . . . . O God, who is cold in slums in winter, whose playmates are rats, from four-legged ones who live with you to two-legged ones who imprison you, help us to touch you.

If that was more than rhetoric, as I believe it was intended to be, then its unconventional vividness might well kindle our empathy for that partnership with God which means in-depth good neighborship with men.

If prayer as empathy does nothing else for us, it

will perpetually remind us of our need to pray for more empathy. Robert Raines, in his *The Secular Congregation,* warns us that "real involvement in the lives and events of our times drives us to acknowledge the limits of our vision and our inability to love our friends, let alone our enemies." And he adds, "As long as we cloister ourselves from the conflicts and tensions of the world, our need of God may remain hidden from us."[4]

In documentation of the point that we need to immerse ourselves in prayer if we are rightly "to love our friends, let alone our enemies," I cite something that Sen. Mark Hatfield of Oregon told a recent graduating class at Princeton Seminary. He said that after he had spoken on the Senate floor in opposition to the Vietnam war, he received a hot letter of protest from an evangelical patriot which began with "Dear former Christian brother . . . ." Thus a courageous expression of social concern and conscience by an eminent Christian statesman evokes an "evangelical" response which in effect "un-brothers" and "un-Christianizes" the senator.

It is difficult to believe that a letter so devoid of empathy was born and bathed in prayer.

Moving one step further, let's think of prayer as *engagement*.

---

4. (New York: Harper & Row, 1968) p. 114.

Prayer as escape is too easy. It is at once too selfish and too sterile.

Prayer as empathy moves us in the right direction. But if it remains just that, it is vision and emotion unfulfilled.

Jesus, as we have seen, not only went to prayer; he went to work. "He went about all the cities and villages, teaching . . . preaching . . . healing."

That is to say, the Jesus who both prescribed and practiced prayer addressed himself to, and became involved in, the needs of the whole man, the body as well as the soul. True, he taught *priority* but never *polarity*. Even the priority was a priority of *value*, not necessarily a priority in *time*. Since he didn't engage in Operation Strait Jacket, he sometimes dealt with the physical need first and then the spiritual, and sometimes he reversed the order.

The point is that he was never a mere theoretician but a practitioner. He was involved.

Centuries later a British missionary went out to Jamaica, felt the dehumanizing viciousness of the institution of slavery, became convinced that its presence was destroying the credibility of the Christians and their gospel, and openly cast his lot with the blacks and the cause of abolition. For this he drew the wrath of the slave owners, both Christian and non-Christian. These persecutors heaped upon him, as one historian put it, "every form of indignity that would be calculated to degrade him in the eyes of the slaves." Church buildings he had erected with limited funds and unlimited courage were burned to the ground.

All of this, far from extinguishing the fire of his social passion, kindled it. He set sail for England in order to stir the fatherland's drowsy conscience on the slavery issue.

> "If I fail in arousing the sympathy of England," he cried, "I will go back to Jamaica and call upon Him who hath made of one blood all nations upon the earth. And if I die without beholding the emancipation of my brethren and sisters in Christ, then, if prayer is permitted in heaven, I will fall at the feet of the Eternal, crying: 'Lord, open the eyes of Christians in England to see the evil of slavery and to ban it from the earth.' "[5]

July 31, 1838, was a memorable day in Jamaica. It was the day when, by an act of the British Parliament, slavery was ended in Jamaica. It was also the beginning of a new thrust forward in evangelism by the churches of the island.

William Knibb, by his involvement on a frontier of social concern, had demonstrated the truthfulness of a tart dictum by Hugh Price Hughes, who said that "the Holy Ghost is not an errand boy for lazy Christians."

Ronald E. Osborn has composed a prayer entitled "California Sunday." In place of *California* you could write in the name of any state in the Union. Here is the prayer:

---

5. Frank Boreham, *A Bunch of Everlastings* (New York: Abingdon, 1920), p. 218.

Once again, O Lord, your day has come,
and we have turned to your house.

We wait here in the holy silence before you,
but out there the beat goes on.

The endless squadrons of the restless crowd the
    freeways,
the sailboats and the cabin cruisers throng the
    waters,
the lawn mowers whir,
and the beat of the world goes on.

All our daily concerns keep drumming with us too,
    O Lord.
We have come here, our God, to worship you,
but we are not very good at spiritual meditation.
So much of everyday's pressure bears down on us
    even here—

the stupid mistake we made on the job,
the tight budget at work and at home,
the way we manage to keep hurting those we
    love,
the burden of unfinished responsibilities,
a nation whose people are set at odds,
the blood that still flows while the war winds
    down,
the fears that clutch at us in the night,
the loneliness that chills our souls when we
least expect.

O God of peace and light, we bow to pray,
and still in our throbbing hearts the beat goes on.

Is there, Lord, no rest for the weary?
even here no calm for our troubled spirits?

Hold us for this moment in your very presence, O
    God,
open our eyes to see you as you really are,
Creator of heaven and this teeming earth,
Lord of history and Savior of sinful men,
Father of the fatherless and brother of all who
    suffer,
and wherever life is most desperate, God with us.

Free us then from any sense of religious failure
because we cannot get the world off our minds.
Help us to see you carrying its griefs on your heart
and sharing the burdens which oppress us every day.

Teach us that true worship which does not close its
    eyes on the world,
but which gives us new sight to see you at work in all
    the confusion.
When we go out from your house to our homes and
    our jobs,
    let us know you there as well as here.

Make us, O God, your saints for the seventies,
no longer fugitives from life as it is
but pilgrims marching to the music of your purpose
out there where the beat goes on.
We pray in the name of Jesus Christ.[6]

---

6. Copyright 1971 Christian Century Foundation. Reprinted by permission from the November, 1971, issue of *The Christian Ministry*.

4

The Biblical Mandate

John H. Yoder

Preface. There are two reasons not to make things easy for ourselves today by simply restating those common convictions which have brought us to this working consultation.

First, it is one of the peculiarities of evangelicalism that the average congregation or the average Christian is trusted to read the Bible for himself. This expectation of immediacy, sometimes spelled out more fully in a doctrine of perspicuity, has its good, strong, gospel reasons. However, it also, when standing alone, has some

Dr. John Howard Yoder, a native of Ohio, is professor of theology and former president of Goshen Biblical Seminary, Elkhart, Indiana. He also teaches theology at nearby Notre Dame. He has served Mennonite relief and mission agencies in Europe, Algeria, Latin America, and Japan. His most recent book is The Politics of Jesus *(Eerdmans, 1972).*

limitations. One is that a person's confidence in the accessibility and the authority of the meaning of Scripture can very soon slip over and take the form of confidence in the adequacy of his own interpretation. How often in recent years we have read articles or have heard sermons on such themes as "the biblical view of . . ." or "the biblical mandate for . . . ." And yet what followed was not an inductive biblical study, was not derived from a particular text, was not the fruit of a new testing of the witness of Scripture, but rather took for granted the general evangelical stance which the communicator already held and knew that his listeners or readers also held, and then related the known values and familiar phrases of that stance to the new question.

The corrective for this is not to deny to the layman the use of the Bible. It is to take serious responsibility for the theologian's task of making visible the structure of interpretation. This is the point of the science of hermeneutics. What is the process which authorizes me to say I am interpreting the biblical view of something or other? Can I go at that in such a way as to claim that my Christian brother or sister should read it the same way?

The second reason is this: Once we have identified the problem of hermeneutics in its historical and linguistic dimensions, we are forced to recognize as well the historic fruits of that problem in the variety of positions held by various Christian traditions, all of which today would be classified as evangelical. Evangelical Anglicans, evangelical Calvinists, evangelical Lutherans, Methodists, Baptists, Mennonites, and Pentecostals each have a different thought structure. Some of the differences have to do with the way we approach the mandate for social concern. It may help us if we face quite openly the fact that there are diverse strategies, and that these strategies operate differently for different purposes with regard to what we ought to do about the varieties of "evangelicalisms."

For some purposes, the differences are downplayed and the parallel focus is accentuated. The common purpose may be publication, evangelism, or the battle against modernism. Often this tendency prevails when a transdenominational meeting of evangelicals is brought together: commonalities tend to be emphasized and diversity played down.

This is fine for program projection and for doing battle, but it is of questionable adequacy when what is needed is to meet a *new* challenge concerning which our several traditions have inherited approaches which genuinely differ from one another.

The obvious alternative is to take the distinctiveness of structure very seriously and to limit cooperation to that which does not in any way jeopardize distinctiveness. This has happened in past debates, when our several movements found their origins. It is a position usually taken again in times of economic or structural retrenchment and often in that kind of psychological retrenchment which is sometimes provoked by the encounter with a new set of challenges for which we do not have answers easily accessible in the tradition.

There might be a third possibility, which would be the expression of one definition of evangelicalism, although different from other traditional definitions. This would be to say that while placing only limited confidence in past answers, either in their commonality or their differences, we trust that in a *renewed* approach to Scripture, in full awareness of the diversity of our approaches, we might find some new light. We might find a *new* way to submit to the bar of Scripture those places where we have traditionally differed, trusting that more careful hermeneutical perspectives drawn from history and language, renewed concern for the shape of the questions the world puts to us, and renewed openness to one another and the Spirit could move us toward a commonality of stance which is not simply the negotiated common denominator of strategy of parallel focus nor static pluralism. It is with a view to laying the groundwork for such a hope that my assignment shall be focused not so much on a mere recital and synthesis of biblical affirmations and commandments as upon dealing with the existent variety of hermeneutical orientations.

The purpose of this typological approach has not been to renew the arguments of history or even to claim to be fully fair to the reality of past argumentation, but rather to refocus the question which we seek to take back to Scripture for new light.

A multiple mandate. We would not be gathered here if we did not believe that the love of a sovereign God drives us into concern for the social order. We would not be gathered here if we were not convinced that the shape of that concern is at least partly a critical one. God does not simply tell us to accept the existing order; he tells us also that it must change. We probably all agree as well that the bindingness and the vitality of our concern for the shape of society will be derived from more than one stream within the salvation story:

To affirm God as a loving Creator, the earth as our home to be stewarded, and the life of our neighbor as entrusted to our care, is one way to say it . . . .

To affirm the covenant with Noah, with its divine protection of life, with its promise of the seasons as the structure of cultural life and divine protection of blood as the presence of personal life, is another . . . .

To affirm the covenant with Abraham, with its call to faith and its promise of a blessing for all the nations, is still another . . . .

To affirm the Mosaic covenant, whose Torah is an abiding testimony to the wholeness of God's concern for the shape of the life of his subjects, is another . . . .

To recount the Hebrew history, with its repeated rhythms of obedience and disobedience, temptation and renewal, is yet another . . . .

To proclaim reconciliation through the blood of the Cross is another . . . .

To respond in faith to the Kingdom proclamation of Jesus as an authoritative reordering of the relationships of those who hear and follow him, and potentially of others as well, is still another . . . .

To recount in faith the story of the apostolic missionary community as it spread a new life-style across the Mediterranean world is another . . . .

To proclaim the hope of a new city whose Builder and Maker is God, where a tree grows whose leaves are for the healing of the nations, is yet another.

All of these drive us into active social concern.

Few of us would declare there must be but one way of stating the mandate for Christian social concern, in only one verbal form, or only one scriptural image.

But that still leaves us with our present agenda. There would not be the need we now acknowledge for a process of common search and formulation, which has not yet been completed, if "Bible-believing Christians" had not somehow in the past failed to put their thoughts together on this subject in a way which would responsibly illuminate their obedience and protect them against the temptation of Constantinian conformity to which we have been especially subject in recent generations.

So the biblical mandate we are to be looking for must be more than the imperative to love the neighbor socially: it must contain a corrective for the tendency to define the neighbor too locally and individualistically. It must not only explain that it is our duty to respect the powers that be, but also provide leverage for formulating the limits of that respect and articulating our resistance when those limits are overrun. It must not simply affirm the obligations of community and of righteousness. It must also equip us to respond when the very structures of community and righteousness become destructive.

All of the themes noted above in passing will be of substantial usefulness in this task. I hope we all affirm them all, even if in different sequences and proportions. My search is for those which can be the most formally constitutive of that understanding of the social task which can provide the instruments of its own self-discipline.

The paradigm of peoplehood. Evangelical preaching and practice in certain classical forms has trusted the will of the regenerate individual to be the bridge between grace and structure. The individual in a position of authority, whose heart has been changed by the gospel, will, it is claimed, use his power more unselfishly, more creatively, more industriously, for good. This is not false, but it is far too small an answer, and one which is more modern than biblical. Among its limitations are the following:

It provides no substantial information about what are the particularly more righteous ways in which power should be used. It must assume either that they are self-evident to the whole society or that they are known somehow intuitively by the converted statesmen. Neither of these assumptions can be supported either by experience or by theology.

It ascribes little significance to the ethical concerns and decisions of people who are not in power.

It fosters the already too great evaluation of coercive power and prestige in society. It makes it still harder than before to put the question whether certain particular powerful positions should exist at all. Certainly, as Frank Buchman argued, if Mussolini had been converted, he would have had great power, which he could have used for good. But if you place your hopes for the welfare of Italy and the glory of God in Italy on the conversion of Mussolini, you are no longer genuinely free to ask whether Fascism is wrong.

It dodges the fact, which a truly honest individual in a high position is very clear about, that many evils are matters of structure and not of inner disposition, so that the most unselfish heart in the world cannot necessarily "use for good" or "clean up" a fundamentally vicious structure.

This approach when taken straight fosters an unevangelical understanding of the *station* or *office* as a relatively autonomous vehicle of moral insight. That the liberty of the Christian man consists of his being released from inauthentic constraints and irrelevant laws, in order to do what belongs to his station, was in the sixteenth century an understandable corrective against clericalism and a potentially useful fulcrum to criticize the crusading glorification of the state as an instrument of divine righteousness. But when taken alone, it is not true. The insight or the role definition of the banker, of the businessman, of the legislator, of the educator is not sufficiently sanctified that he can read off the surface of the social order a definition of the duties of the man of God in that slot, as the celebration of the effectiveness of the sanctified important individual would lead us to try to do.

Now I have suggested that the Christian church as a social reality is the needed corrective. The alternative to the focus on the redeemed individual is not to pay attention only to structures or to massive movements of the mob and the media, but rather to recognize that there is a particular point where the redeemed individual and social structure are both present, namely in the Christian community as a visible body within history. Workshop coordinator Sider, in his instructions, quoted back to me my statement, "The primary social structure through which the gospel works to change other structures is that of the

Christian community."[1] How can it be claimed that the choice of God to work with man in community rather than alone provides correctives for the shortcomings indicated above?

Sometimes the experience of the Christian community is a paradigm in the simple sense. The Christian community does things which the world may imitate. The Christian community feeds the hungry and cares for the sick in a way which may become a model for the wider society. The Christian community makes decisions through group process in which more than one participates, and moves toward decision by consensus rather than by virtue of office and authority. Historians of democracy have seriously suggested that the basis for the concept of the Anglo-Saxon town meeting was the experience of disputation and decision-making in the independent Puritan congregation. Today, even secular business management circles are adopting the concept of decision-making through conversation which stems from the Radical Reformation.

The Christian who does have a position of relative power in the wider society, far from claiming autonomy in that station by virtue of God's having made it an authority unto itself, can be trusted relatively in his role only if he will listen to the admonition of his brethren regarding the way he discharges it. Thus the Christian com-

---

1. John Howard Yoder, *The Politics of Jesus* (Grand Rapids: Eerdmans, 1972), p. 157.

munity is not only a model as community; it is a pastoral and prophetic resource to the person with the responsibilities of office, precisely to keep the office from becoming autonomous as a source of moral guidance. Sometimes the function of the community will be simply to encourage him to have the nerve to do what he already believes is right. At other times, other church members, thanks to their participation in other parts of society, will bring to his attention insights he would have missed; sometimes the community's proclamation of the revealed will of God may provide for him leverage to criticize the present structures.

Serious sociological and psychological analysis should have made it clear to us that there is no such thing as an individual functioning all by himself out of the definition of who his "self" is, standing alone. The person is aware of his being himself and being alone precisely because he is the member of more than one group, and because at some points the claims of several groups upon him conflict. The service of the Christian community to the businessman, the politician, the communicator, the worker, or any other molder of the shape of culture is not to promise and to glorify heroic individual integrity, but rather to provide a reference group which is both accepting and demanding, more reliable and more critical than the other groups and structures in which the socially responsible person is otherwise bound.

The peoplehood which the apostles after Pentecost led in self-understanding called itself the *ekklesia.* That did not mean what *church* means in modern usage: it meant parliament or town meeting, a gathering in which serious business can be done in the name of the Kingdom. In other words the Christian community is a decision-making body, a place where prophetic discernment is tested and confirmed, the organ for updating and applying the understanding of the revealed law of God, the context for the promised further guidance of the Spirit.

Evangelical thought in recent decades has often been hampered by too naive understanding of how the Bible can function authoritatively in social ethics. On the one hand there has been naive trust in the insight of the regenerate man of God; just as naive on the other side has been the trust that a few phrases from the Bible could be translated directly into social policy without any discipline of translation across cultures. The alternatives to these oversimplifications are not relativism or selling out to some contemporary social-science insight, but rather the functioning of the congregation under the guidance of the Spirit. The New Testament does not claim that Scripture contains all the answers. It rather promises us (John 14:25ff, 16:12ff, as samples only) that there will be adequate and binding further guidance given to the church as she goes along, and that this further guidance will be subject to the judgment of the community, oriented by the fixed points of the apostolic witness in the canon.

The peoplehood called *ekklesia* is different

from other peoples in its composition. It includes Jew and Gentile (not simply two ethnic groups but two cultural types). It includes both masters and slaves and makes them brothers "both in the flesh, and in the Lord" (Philemon 16). It includes men and women, replacing their hierarchial relationship in pagan society with mutual subordination (Ephesians 5:21). It shares money and bread and the gifts of the Spirit in a way that is a radical alternative to the authority structures of Gentile society. In all of these respects and more, the Christian community provides both a place to stand from which to say to the world something critically new, and a place to keep testing and exercising the understanding of that critical message.

The Christian community is also a means of influencing other groups. The simple fact that the Church is intractably present on the social scene as a body with her own authority, economic structure, leadership, international relations, openness to new members, conscientious involvement in society at some points and conscientious objection at others, means that social process cannot go on without taking account of her presence and particular commitments.

Permit me to recount a personal experience of a decade ago. We were discussing in an ecumenical conversation circle in Evanston what might be the Christian responsibility for the racially segregated housing picture in that town. The self-evident need, from the point of view of some of the participants in the conversation, was for the ministers of the community to deal with the mayor and city council to ask for municipal administrative measures in favor of open-housing practices. This would be the Church operating, in the person of the ministers, to discharge her social responsibility. The conversation was brought into some disarray when one of us asked whether the real-estate dealers and the sellers of houses were not mostly members of the Protestant churches in Evanston. The answer was that they probably were, but that the preacher was powerless to get his own members to take Christian ethics seriously without the coercion of government to get "the church" *as membership* involved in lay professions to be less un-Christian.

This anecdote is a specimen of the recurrent temptation to expect other forces in society to be more effective, or other authorities to be more insightful, than the body of believers in their structured life together. As Franklin H. Littell analyzed the failure of Prohibition,

> Politicians in the churches attempted to secure by public legislation what they were unable to persuade many of their own members was either wise or desirable . . . . Lacking the authenticity of a genuinely disciplined witness, the Protestant reversion to political action was ultimately discredited, and the churches have not to this day recovered their authority in public life.[2]

---

2. *From State Church to Pluralism* (New York: Doubleday Anchor, 1962) p. 20.

The lesson drawn from the defeat of Prohibition could be that political action against social evils is self-defeating. That would be to misread the point. The point is rather that legislative implementation is only meaningful when it represents the extension of a commitment on the part of the Christian community which has already demonstrated the fruitfulness of that commitment.

I could go on with the list. The Church as a network of complimentary charismata is a laboratory of social pluralism. The Church as educational community is a nurturing ground for counter-cultural values. The Church as community of forgiveness is a live alternative to a society structured around retributive sanctions.

So the foremost political action of God is the calling and creation of his covenant people, anointed to share with him as priests, prophets, and in the servanthood which he revealed to be the human shape of his kingship. The Church is both the paradigm and the instrument of the political presence of the gospel.

But around that center, let us fill out the picture. In seeking to organize what more there is to say, I have followed two formal concepts. One, already stated, is the awareness of past unfaithfulness and failure. This is not an area where we can start simply from the beginning, unfolding either right ideas or right strategies straight out of the Scriptures.

Parenthetically, it might clarify the picture for

us to recognize a tension widely present in evangelicalism between formation and reformation as ways to see oneself. Often the claim is made to be unfolding the truth straight from the center, timeless and unconditional. Yet in actual historic experience, the need has more often been to critique and restore: to admit unfaithfulness and seek renewal. It is this latter view of our task that I assume. I am not asking why Christians should care about the political realm, but why they so often have been involved wrongly. I propose to develop my further outline by itemizing some of the challenges, beginning with the questions, not the answers.

Secondly, I have for this introduction chosen multiplicity, not simplicity. Both preacher and theologian tend to look for one key thought to bring all the rest into line. It could be done. Everything could be seen in the light of creation, or covenant, justification by faith, conversion, love, or hope—or the Church. For two reasons I here avoid the path of simplification:

1. It might invite fruitless denominational debates about whether one center is better than another.

2. It might leave unchallenged the trend to intellectual compartmentalizing, which would see social responsibility as one ministry beside many others, or one good deed beside others, or one chapter of ethics beside others.

I thus willingly pay the price of a certain scattering of my remarks in testimony to the roundedness of what we are trying to describe.

Power is the name of the game. The political realm is the realm of power. Power is the ability to make things happen. The political process channels and distributes this ability. If bad guys have power, bad things will happen. So we good guys must get power to make good things happen. But unfortunately, to get the power for good uses, even the good guys must do some less good things. This way to open the problem leads to some unhelpful blind alleys:

1. It may lead to arbitrariness in judging how much evil is necessary to attain how much good, in which the privilege of person or party rate higher than the competing values.

2. Moral leadership may be replaced by finesse in drawing lines between shades of gray, as estimates of "how much" and "how far" replace "who" and "whether."

3. To say no to the process may seem—to those who say no as well as those who go along— like just another reading on the "how far" kind of question, and as having chosen the purity of noninvolvement as the better part.

I must already object to this analysis as naive political theory. He who in a given situation withdraws or is defeated is not necessarily any less responsible, active, involved, than the one who makes it to the top.

But a deeper cost of the call for the good guys to

get power is the quantifying of what they may sacrifice to get it. The just-war theory quantifies the lives you may take for the sake of some other political good. "National security" justifies the crimes you commit to weaken your critics. The "safety of our troops" justifies unconstitutionally expanding a war. That peace must be "with honor" justifies prolonging a war.

But the focus on the good guys getting control does not first become wrong when they cheat to kill or kill to win. It becomes wrong when control itself is seen as the goal and when power is seen as a neutral quantity easily usable for good. Seen politically, power tends to corrupt: you need no theology to be more realistic than the American mood has been about "government by the people" through their elected representatives.

But you do need the New Testament to see Jesus' alternative: "The kings of the Gentiles lord it over them; and those who have authority over them are called 'Benefactors.' But not so with you . . ." (Luke 22:25, NASB).

Jesus recognizes—as Luke reports it—that "doing good" is a claim the powerful make for themselves. He does not say outright that the claim is false. Nor does he affirm it. He simply sets the issue aside in favor of servanthood as his way to be the expected King, and therefore his disciples' way as well.

But servanthood is not a position of non-power or weakness. It is an alternative mode of power. It is also a way to make things happen, also a way to be present. When we turn from coercion to persuasion, from self-righteousness to service, this is not a retreat but an end run. It brings to bear powers which, on balance, are stronger than the sword alone:

—the power of the truth rediscovered when obscured;

—the power of the dissenter willing to suffer;

—the power of the people to withhold confidence;

—the attraction of an alternative vision;

—the integrity that accepts sacrifice rather than conformity to evil.

We can be protected from absolutizing power for its own sake, and from the betrayals of good causes which such thinking has justified

—by a vision of Christ's servanthood as a live alternative to lordship;

—by awareness of the many other kinds of power on the side of truth and humanness;

—and by realism about the precariousness, the real weakness and the temptations, of the top of the heap.

There's no place like home. Another besetting sin of the political realm is provincialism: the limitation of one's love to one's own kind of people. One of the main reasons Reinhold Niebuhr could rightly say that groups tend to be more selfish than individuals is that a leader's bid for recognition most easily appeals to group interest *against* those of some other class, race, nation . . . .

Narrowness of world awareness may be the fruit of misinformation, of traumatic experiences of migration, or of oppression. A wider than provincial vision may be fostered by education, by travel, and by good experiences with people of other cultures. But the alternative vision which it is our business to proclaim is more than crosscultural education; it is a spiritual mandate. "If anyone is in Christ—there is a whole new world!"

The New English Bible translates 2 Corinthians 5:17 not "a new creature" in the individualistic sense but "a new creation." Paul says that about Jews and Greeks. He says it as well by extension about the divisions between classes and between the sexes. It is just as true by implication of the divisions of tribes and tongues, peoples and nations, which Revelation 5 tells us are overcome by the power of the Lamb that was slain.

We already know, from the development of secular culture, that wider unities are economically and culturally imperative. We have learned to see the region as a wider unity than the village, the nation than the state. But unless the wider vision be spiritually rooted, it will not hold in the crunch against the instincts of group enmity. It is not enough when a few groups join—as in the American melting pot—against a more distant common enemy. Cosmopolitan vision is not enough. Unless the *positive love of the enemy* stands behind the affirmation of the dignity of other groups, unless divisions are transcended by a dynamic rooted in the divine nature (Luke 6:36) and in the reconciling work of Christ (2 Corinthians 5:16ff) it cannot tame our demonic native ethnocentrism.

Refusal to hate or to sacrifice the "enemy" is one safeguard against provincialism, and since our world is already organized in the shape of military nationalisms, our defense must begin there. Yet the Christian offensive focuses at another point, namely, at one more dimension of the peoplehood which we call the mission of the Church. The people of God are by nature a supra- and trans-national reality. Ever since Constantine, Western Christians have been unclear on how and whether Christian brotherhood relativizes national loyalties and identities. Even our overseas missionary efforts have not always been untainted by linkage with the cultural and economic interests of the homeland. The structural looseness of evangelicalism makes it still easier not to hear the voices of our brothers and sisters overseas when they critique the narrowness of our "Christian Americanism." My point is not that we do not care about the rest of the world; the investment in missionary activity shows this clearly enough. But how do we care? Is it to share with them our superior way of life and save them from socialism? Or is it to take counsel with them about what it would mean for us, in the world's most powerful nation, to be accountable beyond our borders?

This may be a good place to stop for a question that goes beyond the Bible itself. Jew and Gentile are reconciled in Christ; but can that "whole new world" be implemented in the political realm? Jesus' disciple will love his enemies: but can that love be imposed on the world? Of course it cannot be imposed; nothing of the meaning of the Christian faith can be imposed upon the unbeliever. But that is not the question. The question is whether, when the Christian acts according to his faith in this way, relativizing provincial selfishness and defending the rights of other parties, he is thereby being apolitical or irrelevant. The answer would seem to be clear: How you see the adversary and the wider human community is the very substance of politics. Love of the enemy and respect for the out-group is not politically *popular,* but it is politically relevant and politically right.

Means and ends: principles or providence. When I speak of what is "right," I have identified another abiding issue; what is the place of pragmatic compromise? Are "right" and "wrong" timeless and clear? Or situational and calculating? The justification for specific political activities which are not evidently expressive of the love of God and immediately productive for the welfare of the neighbor is usually given in terms of calculation of the projected effects of a given action or of the evil events which would take place if such questionable actions were not taken.

To use a traditional label, contemporary political ethical thinking is practically without exception "utilitarian." The structure of a utilitarian calculation may be complex or simple, long- or short-range. One may speak immediately of some particular threat to be warded off, or one may use long-range prudential considerations like "Honesty is the best policy" or "I do not want to be responsible for the erosion of the constitutional prerogatives of my office."

Utilitarianism as a style in ethics is so prevalent in our culture as to be hardly challengeable. It would be too long to argue carefully here the philosophical inadequacy of simple utilitarianism as an ethical system.[3]

---

3. Among the logical shortcomings of utilitarianism as a full system are the following:

Effectiveness in reaching a goal can be measured only if the goal itself has been justified by some other criterion than utility, and if the price that must be paid for reaching the goal can also be quantified in terms that reach beyond the situation in order to permit weighing the price and the goal against each other.

There is a hidden nonutilitarian assumption when I say, "I *should* make the course of events come out right."

Dealing with the *effects* of a decision in terms of causal process presupposes a closed causal system permitting me to evaluate my action in terms of its predictable results; yet the fact that I am making a decision whose effects have not been calculated assumes in my own person an openness within the system. If I am to take seriously that the system is open where *I* make *my* decision (even if it be on the basis of my calculation of utility), I can hardly justify assuming that all the other agents within the system are completely docile to mechanistic causation.

He who phrases an issue in terms of the tension between

Right now, as this nation rehearses daily the destructive effects upon our community of the liberties taken by those who felt that whatever they needed to do for the sake of a very good cause was justified, we have again begun to see the human side of the argument for a morality of principle. But now our question is the narrower one. Is there anything particular about the biblical message, or about evangelical Protestantism which could speak with a fitness of its own to this question? Does biblical theology push us toward a particular mood or structure in ethics, as well as setting basic ethical norms?

I suggest that it does, and that one element of the correction for a self-justifying and self-accrediting pragmatism is a mood of *doxology* or trust, in which believing behavior is seen as an effect and not only a cause. Right action is a reflection of a victory already won as much as it is a contribution to a future achievement. It is more an act of praise rather than of simple servile obedience. We do not enter responsibly into the structures of social concern because we are sure of

---

"impersonal principles" and "effectiveness toward good goals in the situation" thereby obfuscates another basic ethical dimension: that of the agent of decision. The language of "principle"—whatever its limits—at least safeguards the concept of accountability beyond oneself. The justification in terms of projected results on the other hand tends to assign to the agent himself both projection and evaluation. What the Watergate burglars and the Plumbers said was "Legality is less important than national security"—a formally perfect example of pragmatic reasoning. But what they said in fact was "We are accountable to no one."

what we can get done there, but because we are proclaiming the lordship of Christ and predicting the day when every knee will bow before him. Thus our conviction and our commitment are not dependent on our predictable effectiveness, nor on our confidence in our analysis of the mechanisms which we are attempting to manipulate. I do not mean to suggest any lack of concern for the study of the structures and the mechanisms of social change; but we do not canonize our interpretation of those structures in such a way that it could at certain times tell us to do the wrong thing for a good cause. If we saw our obedience more as praising God and less as running his world for him, we would be less prey to both despair and disobedience.

Another side of the corrective for self-serving pragmatism is the ancient Hebrew denunciation of idolatry. Idolatry means the willingness to honor, and to sacrifice for, other values, other loyalties than God himself. Radical monotheism exorcizes the spirit of compromise by challenging the merit of the causes which are absolutized when truth, or life, or health are sacrificed to them. But idolatry means more than that. The difference between the true God and an idol is not only that one is worthy of honor and the other not. The idolater uses his prayer and offerings to manipulate the powers of fertility and strength. The Canaanite did not sacrifice to Baal because Baal was holy, worthy, or righteous. His cult was for the sake of his culture. Ancient Near Eastern idolatry, in other words, was the pragmatism of that age. The gods were used for human purposes, whereas Yahweh was to be honored for his own sake.

None of these considerations sets aside the need to think, to weigh the likely effects and the relative costs of available strategies. But they may help diminish the arbitrariness, the self-confidence, and the shortsightedness with which deeper values tend to be given up for apparent immediate effect.

Reverence for language. When the Decalogue forbids the false oath, and when Jesus "fulfills" the law by forbidding all oaths, this is by no means a ritualistic taboo or inexplicable prescription which only the finicky and legalistic will respect and the more enlightened may properly authorize themselves to pass over. We must rather learn to see here a double truth:

—the fragility of all human relations, depending as they do on words which may be distorted, colored, and on commitments which may be broken;

—the self-giving divine presence to recreate and guarantee reliability of language. In a kind of type of the incarnation to come, Yahweh comes among men, putting at our mercy the mystery of his name, subject to our misuse, inviting our respect. Jesus extends that same care over the rest of our language.

Open, true communication in place of the fabrication and management of information is a prerequisite of social health. Truth-telling as moral ultimate is rooted in God's own nature; truth-telling as social *sine qua non* has yet to be firmly anchored even in the most civilized democracies. When a press secretry can without apology declare his prior statements "inoperative," when an ethos of secrecy is so self-evident that "leaks" to the public are considered a worse offense than the misdeeds they betray, we see again the need for what Jesus meant when, sweeping away all asseverations as coming "from the evil one," he simplified and sanctified words: "Let yes be yes and no no."

Postscript. This should be sufficient to exemplify—though not to exhaust—my claim that many strands of Christian faith point us into responsible, distinctive social presence, and that we may find our way farther and faster if we begin—rather than starting "from scratch" or "ideally"—with what has obviously gone wrong:

    —individualism in faith and ethics,
    —the search for power,
    —pragmatism as a justification,
    —provincialism,
    —the abuse of communication.

I have left to one side—because it does not arise in the Bible itself—the issue which historical theology calls "spiritualism"; the idea that religious reality is best identified—or safe-guarded—by fencing it off from the real world, whether in the "heart," in mystical "insight," or revealed mysteries. Then the transition from the spiritual realm to the social or from being to doing is a new problem. The problem *is* real; for some of us, and for more of our evangelical constituencies, it is the first question. But it is not a problem in the Bible. It is the product of our post-biblical experience, and therefore it belongs only at the edge of my assignment. To deal with it we would have to move into historical and systematic theology. Creation, covenant, incarnation, reconciliation, Kingdom, Church—all the major biblical themes are rooted socially in common history.

I have dealt with form more than content, with the why of social concern more than the what. I have not itemized liberation, violence, peace, economic justice, productivity, ecology . . . not that the Bible would not speak as well to these matters of content: it certainly does. But what has been holding us apart from one another and holding us away from the task has been the debates about the *whether* rather than unclarity about the *what,* and because the *what* will vary according to context. The *why* is the same hope as of old; but a hope whose fulfillment we claim Jesus began:

It shall come to pass in the latter days
   that the mountain of the house of the Lord
shall be established as the highest of the mountains,

and shall be raised up above the hills;
and peoples shall flow to it,
   and many nations shall come, and say:
"Come, let us go up to the mountain of the Lord,
   to the house of the God of Jacob;
that he may teach us his ways
   and we may walk in his paths."
For out of Zion shall go forth the law,
   and the word of the Lord from Jerusalem.
He shall judge between many peoples,
   and shall decide for strong nations afar off;
and they shall beat their swords into plowshares,
   and their spears into pruning hooks;
nation shall not lift up sword against nation,
   neither shall they learn war any more;
but they shall sit every man under his vine and under
      his fig tree,
   and none shall make them afraid;
   for the mouth of the Lord of hosts has spoken.
                              (Micah 4:1-4, RSV)

5

Reflections

Frank S. Gaebelein

The Thanksgiving Workshop made an important, though long overdue, beginning in the forthright expression of greater social concern on the part of evangelicals. That such a varied and transdenominational gathering, after two days of rigorous and sometimes unsparing discussion, succeeded in forging and, with near unanimity, agreeing on a declaration that goes well beyond what has been said on social matters by any comparable evangelical group—this was an event of genuine significance.

To be sure, the workshop did not accomplish everything that had been hoped for. So much time was spent on the declaration that the few remaining hours were manifestly inadequate for responsible consideration of the extensive agenda of specific proposals for action. Yet while the meeting ended with unfinished business of vital importance, it did so, I believe, for the right reason. For a succinct statement of evangelical social concern had first of all to be thought through and adopted as a basis for more faithful discipleship in this area. The workshop, therefore, should be viewed as having been adjourned to the one now being planned for 1974. This second meeting will afford participants the opportunity of considering practical steps evangelicals can take to implement their social concern.

On the personal level, the 1973 workshop proved to be far more than just another conference. Much of its value lay in the acceptance and respect we felt for one another as we recognized our common commitment to the Lord Jesus Christ and the Scriptures and to a fuller expression of our own discipleship. Though we were a highly diverse group and though our encounter was at times intense and stressful, we experienced a warmth of fellowship that culminated in a moving time of worship in our final session. Indeed, many of us felt that the Lord had graciously been with us.

Special recognition is due the younger leadership on the planning committee, because they had the vision for the workshop and the courage and initiative to make it a reality. As one of the older generation of evangelicals who was there, I am grateful for the privilege of taking part in a memorable and rewarding experience.

Frank S. Gaebelein, a former coeditor of Christianity Today, *is headmaster emeritus of the Stony Brook School on Long Island.*

Samuel Escobar

For a Latin American evangelical, a typical product of British missions who has gone through the post-missionary identity crisis, the meeting in Chicago was specially meaningful. The presence of veterans of evangelical causes like Rees, Gaebelein, Henry, Ramm, and Yoder provided for me a sense of the historical in the crowded meeting room of the YMCA Hotel.

As I watched faces there, my mind went back to my early university days in Lima, when I read with real joy in an Argentine ecumenical magazine about a book called *The Uneasy Conscience of Modern Fundamentalism* and a man called Carl Henry. I also recalled the midnight dialogues of Union Seminary students from Buenos Aires in a World Vision conference in Cordoba, crowded around Bernard Ramm, the unusual "conservative" they had met. (These same students had quarrelled that very morning with Bob Pierce for his staunch defense of U.S. involvement in Korea and Vietnam.) I recalled also my talk with Paul Rees and some leftist students in a cafe in downtown Cochabamba, and the passionate interest of Brazilian and Argentine students in their encounter with John H. Yoder in Cordoba and Campinas some years ago. And to see all these brethren together, some of them meeting for the first time, was remarkable indeed, at least for me.

The painful search for balanced sentences in a declaration is a process through which I have been going since I represented my school at the Peruvian Federation of University Students. But in the context of an evangelical gathering the pain goes deeper. It does not come so much from the rational effort to build bridges instead of walls with our words as from the shocking realization that maybe our people—our evangelical rank and file—are not ready for some truth at all. It is not only that a huge dose would prove to be fatal, but that just a drop will be too much. After all, maybe evangelical declarations have to be balanced; it is left for biblical epistles to be passionate—James dixit, Paul dixit.

A step is a step. What we must avoid now is the temptation to make the declaration nothing but an "interesting" outburst from a group of *enfants terribles* that the evangelical community can afford to have. During a convention some time ago, a missionary friend of mine told me that evangelicals have come to the point of having as part of their program an act of masochism. They let radical speakers come and talk, and after an adequate dose of verbal abuse which they stoically accept, they then carry on business as usual. Structures are not touched. Presuppositions are not criticized.

It is a matter of prayer and action. Prayer

first, because as with real revival, there is no formula that produces it mechanically. And obedience to the Lord in relation to the social implications of the gospel is first a matter of the Spirit of God moving among his people. That is already happening. Models exist here and there. They are still small, experimental, and constantly threatened, but even in Chicago we heard of some of them. Signs that the Spirit is blowing? May He give us clean eyes and clean ears. Action also is needed. A way must be found for the ferment to run. I hope we will not go the elitist path that the ecumenical theologians and leaders have gone. If these ideas do not get to the people, they will die in the ivory tower. We have to fight so that people will look at them, sing them, be dressed by them, and then be possessed by them. And maybe our efforts in that very direction will prove whether the evangelical body is a sick man who can be healed or a colossal corpse that is organized, regimented and mobilized by expert manipulators.

Perhaps the crunch will come at the point that Anabaptist theologians are making with renewed vigor. Maybe it is not enough to correct the system, to add some spiritual flavor to it, to dig a hole for an evangelical presence in it. Maybe it is necessary to question it and disengage ourselves from it. Maybe developments are calling us evangelicals also to attempt an escape from the Constantinian captivity of the Church—not into Marxism dressed with the rhetoric of liberation theology, but into a New Testament Christianity that takes seriously again what it means to call *Jesus* and *only Jesus*—not Mammon—Lord.

Samuel Escobar is general director of Inter-Varsity Christian Fellowship—Canada.

On the issue of women's role in church and society, the Thanksgiving Workshop was a consciousness-raising session.

All participants seemed ready and eager to confess their personal sins and the church's shortcomings in relation to racial minorities. But few were nearly so inclined even to recognize the sexism inherent in our social institutions.

Some were almost totally unaware of the issues. No woman was included on the steering committee to plan the conference. Several women were, however, among the participants and on the program. Perhaps illustrative of the level of awareness was the fact that "Dr. Ruth Bentley" was listed as a participant, but as chairperson for an afternoon session she became "Mrs. William Bentley."

Sexism appeared only tangentially in the four-page original draft of the declaration presented by the committee. Only after lengthy debate did the workshop accept the statement "We acknowledge that we have encouraged men to prideful domination and women to irresponsible passivity. So we call on both men and women to practice mutual submission and active discipleship."

The first sentence caused only a ripple of

concern, but repeated attempts were made to soften, subvert, or side-step the second—particularly the phrase "mutual submission."

Conservatives were unconvinced by texts like "Be subject to one another out of reverence for Christ" (Ephesians 5:21) that men were to be in any way submissive. Friends of the women's movement were wary that many would ignore the "mutual" and see the statement as supporting traditional male dominance and female subjection. But in the end all were convinced that the statement was a proper expression of Christian biblical concern.

The conference also passed several action proposals submitted by a women's caucus composed of both men and women. The group called for a critical restudy of secular sex roles and "our hermeneutical principles regarding the interaction of Scripture and culture." They asked the church to revise Sunday school and other teaching materials in order to present less stereotyped pictures of male-female relationships. And in the area of economics another resolution urged Christian organizations to set a pattern for the world rather than simply waiting to comply with government orders concerning equality of women in hiring, pay, and promotion.

The future of such proposals and the work of the conference in general will depend on reactions to it by churches, other evangelical leaders, and concerned individuals. Hopefully the workshop will have several lasting effects on the church's view of women.

First of all, Christian leaders, 99.44 percent of them male, will perhaps become more self-conscious. They may begin to think twice before excluding women from planning and participation—though getting beyond token representation may take some time. Concurrently, women may begin to use the gifts the Holy Spirit has given them to get the necessary credentials and try to work their way up in Christian organizations where their voices can be heard.

More importantly, however, the declaration may spur Christians to reflect on the way men and women do interact in our society and the changes our faith should make in those relationships. What does it mean to follow Jesus Christ, who freely accepted women disciples, who encouraged their theological inquiry, who insisted that women's biological and cultural functions should be subservient to serving God, who first revealed his resurrection to women and commanded them to tell the world?

And what are we to make of Paul's decree that Jews and Gentiles were to live and worship as equals because "there is neither Jew nor Greek, . . . slave nor free, . . . male nor female; for you are all one in Christ Jesus" (Galatians 3:28)?

The Thanksgiving Workshop was one of the first occasions on which a group of conservative Christian leaders was obliged to take the issue of women's rights seriously. It will not be the last. They faced the problem with a fair degree of honest searching and Christian charity. My prayer is that the spirit of this beginning will grow and blossom among all Christians.

Nancy Hardesty, formerly assistant editor of Eternity *and assistant professor at Trinity College, is now working toward the Ph.D. at the University of Chicago Divinity School.*

Carl F.H. Henry

The Thanksgiving '73 "Declaration of Evangelical Social Concern" was significant for numerous reasons, some of which I shall indicate below.

Its importance for the future doubtless depends upon whether evangelical Christians can marshal cooperation for certain social objectives even as they do for evangelistic goals, whether some independent spirits make it an occasion of provocatory reaction, or whether others unilaterally exploit the statement for partisan purposes. No single evangelical enterprise or leader—whether *Christianity Today* or evangelist Billy Graham or whatever and whoever— today speaks definitively for evangelical social concern. Reasons for this are not hard to give, but no profitable purpose would be served by listing them here.

There is no doubt that the American evangelical outlook today is more disposed to social involvement than it has been for two generations. Yet those who have direct access to evangelical masses have not been providing principal leadership for authentic courses of action. This accommodates a great deal of confusion, the more so since ecumenical spokesmen, Carl McIntire, and others have successfully exploited mass-media coverage for conflicting positions that often have more support in emotion than in sound reason.

Whatever disposition some interpreters may have to shrug off the Chicago Declaration as saying nothing that has not already been said by denominational or ecumenical commissions on social action, negatively at least it avoided several mistakes to which contemporary religious activism has been highly prone. For some denominational spokesmen, changing social structures constitutes the Church's evangelistic mission in the modern world; the call to the new birth in the context of a miraculous redemption—whether under the umbrella of Graham crusades, the Jesus movement, Key '73, or whatever—was considered a diversionary waste of time, energy, and money. The sole change demanded by the god of the social radicals is in social structures, not in individuals. The Chicago evangelicals, while seeking to overcome the polarization of concern in terms of personal evangelism or social ethics, also transcended the neo-Protestant nullification of the Great Commission.

A second defect of ecumenical social engagement has been its failure to elaborate the revealed biblical principles from which particular programs and commitments must flow if they are to be authentically scriptural. Insofar as the Chicago Declaration spoke, it attempted to do so in a specifically biblical way. The cleft between the ecumenical hierarchy and the laity, along with many clergy as well, derived in part from pervasive doubt that publicly approved sociopolitical particulars could actually be derived from "Christian ethics," "the Church," "the Cross," or whatever other spiritual flag was hoisted by religious lobbyists. Instead of being rallied to support specific legislative or social positions in view of hierarchical approval, a generation of church-goers illiterate in scriptural principles of social ethics ought to have been nurtured in scriptural teaching and urged to seek a good conscience in applying the biblical principles to contemporary situations.

The Chicago Declaration did not leap from a vision of social utopia to legislative specifics, but concentrated first on biblical priorities for social change. A high responsibility presently rests on evangelical clergy to deepen the awareness of churchgoers—and their own expertise as well—in what the Bible says about social morality.

The Chicago Declaration sought to transcend the polarization of "right" and "left" by concentrating not on modern ideologies but on the social righteousness that God demands. To be sure, Chicago participants reflected a variety of perspectives, and many differences remain on specifics. Most of the biting social criticism of the twentieth century has been left to Marxists; this creates a climate in which Marxist solutions gain a hearing and prestige wider than they would have were they not permitted to preempt a field to which the ancient biblical prophets spoke boldly in a time when pagan kings were thought to be incarnate divinities and to rule by divine right.

The paramount Chicago concern was not to advance one or another of the current ideologies but to focus on the divine demand for social and political justice, and to discover what the Kingdom of God requires of any contemporary option. In brief, the Chicago evangelicals did not ignore transcendent aspects of God's Kingdom. Nor did they turn the recognition of these elements into a rationalization of a theology of revolutionary violence or of pacifistic neutrality in the face of blatant militarist aggression. Neither did they trumpet such fanfare as "capitalism can do no wrong" or "socialism is the hope of the masses." The real interest was in the question: What are the historical consequences of the economic ideologies for the masses of mankind?

To speak now of positive significance, one striking feature of the Chicago Declaration is the very fact of evangelical initiative in social action at a time when the secular and ecumenical social thrust is sputtering for lack of steam. Ecumenical activism accelerated to the peak of massive public demonstrations mounting direct political pressures upon Congress and the White House, at times involving civil disobedience and disruptive tactics. Failure of these power techniques to achieve effective social changes has understandably led to a disenchantment with public institutions, instead of reexamination of ecumenical policies, practices, and proposals for swift solution.

Evangelicals are contemplating anew the Evangelical Awakening, which is often said to have spared England the throes of the French Revolution. In that movement of social morality, evangelicals took an initiative in such matters as slavery, factory working conditions, child labor laws, illiteracy, prison conditions, unemployment, poverty, education for the underprivileged, and much else. If ever America has stood in dire need of an awakening of both social and personal morality, the moment is now.

Another promising center of the Chicago conference was its interest in the problem of power and politics. Evangelicals see no promising way into the future of the nation unless the political scene reflects the participation of those who are involved for reasons higher than self-interest, a kind of political involvement now too much at a premium. While there is no disposition to launch an "evangelical political party," there is mounting concern for open evangelical engagement in the political arena.

If evangelical leadership means anything identifiable, it ought to imply at least that one's public moral responses in time of crisis are highly predictable. Sad to say, it does not always work out that way. But if it works out with a high degree of probability, the national scene could take a happy turn for the better.

Carl F. H. Henry wrote the above for the March 1, 1974, issue of Christianity Today, *the magazine he edited for more than a decade.*

Implicit in the Chicago Declaration, as I interpret it, is the conviction that Christian life in God's world is wider than merely personal or even ecclesiastical. It is social, political, economic as well. Sin, the declaration implies, is structural and institutional as well as personal. Likewise redemption means to save more than our souls. Christ saves our *lives,* our relationships, even as they become organized in social institutions. Poverty, in other words, cannot be dismissed simply as the sign of some poor person's sinful living. Rather, poverty is most often institutionally established by the very structure of our cities, our economy, our politics, our patterns of control and distribution of the resources God built into the earth.

The discovery of such a high level of biblically spirited consensus on social justice among such a diverse collection of people was to me a surprise and an immensely satisfying experience. I shall be happy if the perspective and concerns expressed by the handful of academics, church officials, and editors present in Chicago can now begin to find wider community among the world of laborers, tradesmen, managers, professionals, housewives, shopkeepers, and farm workers who help make up the Body of Christ.

My remark has a point. The Christian churches, whose people gather for worship on Sun-
days, must surely proclaim the Word of God for
justice, stewardship, and social well-being. But
for the rest of the week, all of us as God's people
are mandated to find ways actually to implement
such things. Those of us who work within industry, trade, finance, agriculture, and government and political institutions must work for
justice and economic stewardship in the very
context of these vocations themselves. And all of
us who buy goods and secure services and who
may vote as citizens must do the same in these activities. Justice and stewardship are no sideline
concerns but the responsibility of all of us within
the everyday course of our work and living.

Can we not find ways to *communally* implement justice and stewardship as God's people,
with shared and collective responsibility and action? Not merely as individual persons in isolation
from each other, not as the institutional church
per se, but as God's people acting together in
various ways. For example, cannot the Christian
Business Men's Committee International expand
its attention beyond personal evangelism, Bible
study, and moral tone, and begin to study ways to
exercise Christian leadership within business and
industry on the questions of production, work,
use of resources, distribution of goods, wages,
pricing, quality of product, advertising? Cannot they, like the rest of us, in other words, bring
their Christian commitments to bear upon the

very matters that lie at the center of their vocation as men of business?

Christians from many other traditions—Catholic and ecumenical—are also awakening to the biblical mandate for full-orbed Christian life. Cannot those called evangelical become more open to the new lines of identity now emerging in response to God's Word? Cannot the older lines of demarcation within Christendom become relativized under the fresh impact of biblical renewal? We must be aware that the convictions and hopes of the Chicago Declaration are shared by more Christians than evangelicals.

I hope that God will open the whole lives of his people to the *shalom* of Christ's redemption for the affairs of the whole creation.

C.T. McIntire is a professor at Toronto's Institute for Christian Studies.

Although decades late, the declaration is nevertheless significant, if for no other reason than that it could herald the end of the beginning of white evangelical involvement in the pressing social issues of our day. The almost ever presence of war, the moral decline in the forces of domestic government (including the presidency), the economic issues that negatively affect the growing numbers of the poor while simultaneously favoring the rich and super-rich, the oppressive mechanisms by which the nonwhite nations are being exploited—and here at home, the most pressing issue of them all, the worsening racial situation—these cry out, as they always have, for God's justice to be expressed through his people.

Up to now, white evangelical response has certainly not been proportionate to the seriousness of the situation. Too often and too much, the sound of silence has been the major voice lifted up as evangelicals fled from what they insisted on calling "the social gospel." At Chicago, hopeful signs that this might be coming to an end have appeared. Foot-shuffling, side-stepping, and relaxing in the status quo have been challenged at last.

It is true that some of us, both black and white,

felt that portions of the declaration could have been more explicitly stated. Blacks especially had to press aggressively for a strong statement on the complicity of white evangelicalism in the individual manifestations and group mechanisms that originated and perpetuate racial oppression in America. We felt that while racial prejudice and discrimination are not the only social issues that plague America and her churches, it is the one above all others that colors all others. In America it determines more than anything else where a man shall live, whether or not he shall work, and the quality of education he will have the opportunity to obtain. To be prophetic in international relations is much easier than to play the role of drum major for justice at home. That is why we felt that a serious declaration of self-recognition and repentance must be forthcoming, or else we could not be signatories to the document. And although the declaration would not be adequate for a purely black constituency, it has to be, in my judgment, about the strongest that has so far come from white evangelicalism. To be sure, individuals, and some groups, within the white community have already made their voices heard; a beginning has therefore been made. Our fervent hope and prayer is that this declaration will signal the end of the beginning. As Marvin Gaye says, "Let's get it on!"

William H. Bentley is president of the National Black Evangelical Association.

Paul B. Henry

The Workshop on Evangelicals and Social Concern was significant for several reasons. First, the breadth of representation at the workshop signaled the fact that the major leaders of mainline evangelicalism are conscious of the apostasy in the evangelical community in failing to articulate the social and political claims of the gospel. The attack on the social indifference of evangelicalism no longer comes from just a minority of prophetic critics within evangelical circles or from those outside the evangelical community.

Second, the make-up of the workshop gives a clue to the structure of evangelical leadership for the coming generation. Just as Elijah passed the mantle of leadership to Elisha, so, too, the patriarchs of contemporary evangelicalism (Gaebelein, Henry, Jones, Rees, etc.) gave their blessing to a broad spectrum of younger evangelicals who had initiated the gathering. Significantly, this younger group represented a diversity of perspectives and backgrounds unusual in traditional evangelical gatherings, including articulate blacks, women, and political activists.

Third, the declaration issued at the workshop was different from the usual ecclesiastical resolutions of this genre. It was rooted in the authority of biblical injunctions and addressed itself to the Christian community, calling for repentance resulting in good works done to the glory of God. It was not a political tract calling any particular party or government into question. Rather, it was a bill of impeachment passed upon the evangelical church itself.

Thus, it puts the blame and the remedy for our social evils right where they belong—on the shoulders of the 40 million evangelicals in this country. If we can't solve the problem of racism in our own churches, what right do we have to pontificate to the rest of the world? If we can't place our loyalty to the demands of God over and above our loyalty to the nation, how can we truly call ourselves soldiers of the Cross? And if we can't divest ourselves of our captivity to suburban, materialistic American culture, how can we speak to the maldistribution of wealth in our country and around the world?

But for all that was accomplished at the workshop, there is still much which needs to be done. Evangelicals need to establish a list of priorities for social and political action. And they need to develop unified strategies and programs for concrete social and political engagement. The workshop failed to deal with the problems—both ethical and practical—of political power. These unanswered questions point to the need for more gatherings of this sort. Otherwise we may have done nothing more than engage in religious flagellation devoid of any real commitment to reaching the world for Christ.

Paul B. Henry is assistant professor of political science at Calvin College.

Many American Christians, who had come to identify closely with American political and economic power and prestige and with this administration in particular, felt confused, angered, and betrayed by the revelations of Watergate. Biblical theology alone should have brought us to a more realistic and critical view of the state and its institutions. We should have been much more alert to the dangers of close identification with and uncritical allegiance to governmental power. Our recent history should have demonstrated to us the growing abuse and injustice of the political and economic insitutions of American life and society.

The most important result from the Watergate episode would not be the impeachment of government officials. Rather, it would be the hope of lessons learned by the Church about its responsibilities, about its mission in this society. Watergate should be viewed as a blessing in that it brought the truth to light. If the revelations help us to rediscover our biblical roots and to reexamine our recent history, it might serve to help the Church be more obedient to its calling.

A very hopeful sign which pointed to that possibility occurred at a gathering of fifty evangelical leaders over Thanksgiving weekend, 1973. The *Chicago Sun-Times* referred to the event as a "historic workshop" and suspected that it might ultimately be regarded as the most important church-related event of the year.

The workshop and declaration reflect the new stirrings and directions in the evangelical church, one of the largest religious groupings in the country. New movements toward costly discipleship and social justice have been occurring which directly challenge the credibility of those religious figures who serve as chaplains to the status quo.

Those of us who gathered in Chicago represented a broad spectrum of evangelical leadership: young and old, black and white, male and female, denominational and ecumenical. But we developed a common spirit at many points as we proceeded. All felt the urgent priority of Christian response to the crisis of American wealth and power. The declaration has been given much attention in major evangelical publications and other segments of the religious press and is attracting growing support.

The event pointed to the fact that the message of radical discipleship is being heard. The workshop, along with other recent events, point to the emergence of a "biblical radicalism." Many are coming to believe that the gospel of Jesus Christ is indeed a radical message: in its demand for personal transformation, in its spiritual and intellectual power, and in its dynamic ethic that drives toward social justice. The call to discipleship is a call to break, in a fundamental way, with the values, the mind-set, the conformist patterns of our society. This call is especially urgent for those of us in the heart of the wealthiest, most powerful, and most violent nation on earth. The greatest need is for an obedient and prophetic Church. We need those willing to turn in repentance, to live in resistance, to practice reconciliation, to seek justice, to create alternatives.

With the decline of the New Left and other movements for social change present in the sixties, along with the spreading radical Christian consciousness, it is highly probable that the strongest thrusts toward prophetic witness and social justice may well spring from those whose faith is Christ-centered and unapologetically biblical.

Jim Wallis is editor of the Post-American.

Dale W. Brown

Though I consider my identity with those who strive to be biblically faithful, for the most part I have remained an outsider in relation to the so-called evangelical movement. Art Gish and Jim Wallis led me to an awareness of growing numbers of evangelicals who believe a call to radical discipleship to be an integral part of conservative faith. For this reason, I welcomed the opportunity to participate in the Thanksgiving gathering. It was inspiring to observe the high Christian quality of evangelical leadership committed to proclaim Christ *and* his Kingdom of righteousness, justice, and peace.

My pilgrimage of faith had found me a part of a great variety of social-action efforts, committees of the American Friends Service Committee, work camps, and the vicissitudes of the peace and civil-rights movements. While sharing a common biblical vision of the coming of God's Kingdom with many, I grew increasingly aware of the major pitfalls of liberal social action. These were often manifested in a naive analysis of problems, an overly optimistic assumption that the world will easily be won to Christ's way, a refusal to recognize the depth of human sin and evil, the elitist tendency to manipulate structures from the top in the name of helping all, and the propensity of compromising the Christian way in order to be "realistic" and "responsible."

Because of my pilgrimage, it was natural that there were times during the gathering when I became fearful that the evangelicals might imbibe many of the same errors of the liberals. Likewise, there was a real temptation at times to adopt a patronizing stance in listening to the Johnny-come-lately concerns about racism, sexism, imperialism, and militarism. I even wondered during the fascinating debate about the meaning of the word *evangelical* whether these evangelicals of today were destined to become the liberals of tomorrow, even as many of the liberals of today represent the cut-flower specimens of conservative rootage. Nevertheless, I was moved and filled with hope. My prayer of hope is that God will use these dedicated and committed servants and our prophetic statement for the breaking in of his way and will into the history of our time. May there be a powerful social witness and vision in the seventies anchored deeply in his Word.

Dale W. Brown is a former moderator of the Church of the Brethren.